COACHING

Disabled Performers

ISBN: 1 902523 60 1

First Edition
Author: Annie Kerr
Editors: Penny Crisfield and Chris Rigg
Designer: Debbie Backhouse

Second Edition
Authors: Annie Kerr and Ian Stafford
Editor: Laura Graham
Sub-editor: Helen Bushell
Designer: Sandra Flintham

Photos courtesy of actionplus sports images.

sports coach UK would like to thank Dr Jennifer Davies, Medical Adviser to the Down's Syndrome Association, for her input into the second edition.

The Inclusion Spectrum is reproduced with the kind permission of the English Federation of Disability Sport.

sports coach UK
114 Cardigan Road
Headingley
Leeds LS6 3BJ
Tel: 0113-274 4802 Fax: 0113-275 5019
E-mail: coaching@sportscoachuk.org
Website: www.sportscoachuk.org

Patron: HRH The Princess Royal

Published on behalf of
sports coach UK by

Coachwise Solutions
Coachwise Ltd
Chelsea Close
Off Amberley Road
Armley
Leeds LS12 4HP
Tel: 0113-231 1310 Fax: 0113-231 9606
E-mail: enquiries@coachwisesolutions.co.uk
Website: www.coachwisesolutions.co.uk

Preface

If you are already coaching disabled people or would like to do so, this resource is for you. It is assumed that you already have some coaching experience and much of this existing experience and knowledge will prove readily applicable to coaching disabled people. This comprehensive guide will help you to decide if, and how, you might need to adjust your coaching practice to meet their specific needs.

This resource has been written to support a three hour workshop of the same name. It builds on the material in *How to Coach Disabled People in Sport* (previously known as *Working with Disabled Sportspeople*) and its associated two hour workshop. The aim of both this resource and workshop is to increase the numbers and enhance the expertise of coaches working with disabled people and subsequently increase the opportunities available for disabled people to participate in sport and develop their skills. Each Chapter provides information, activities and questions to help you check your own understanding.

You are strongly recommended to attend the accompanying workshop, where there will be an opportunity to discuss key principles and issues with coaches from other sports. Where these workshops are run for one specific sport, there may be opportunities for hands-on practical coaching experience. For details of workshops in your area, telephone **sports coach UK** on 0113-274 4802, or find details of your local regional office on the website at www.sportscoachuk.org

Key to symbols used in the text

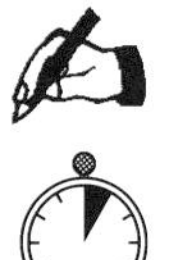 An activity.

Approximate length of time to be spent on the activity.

- Throughout this resource, the pronouns he, she, him, her and so on are interchangeable and intended to be inclusive of both males and females. It is imortant in sport, as elsewhere, that both genders have equal status and oportunities.
- Although the emphasis of this resource is on coaching, it is aimed at all those who lead or deliver sports programmes (eg coaches, leaders, teachers, instructors, development officers, officials, administrators, volunteers, parents/carers) and those with responsibility for the organisation of sport (eg national governing bodies, local authorities, centre managers, sports clubs).
- All information is correct at time of publication.

Contents

CHAPTER 1

Introduction

1.0 What's In It For You?

You will probably have one aim in mind as you work through this resource – to improve your ability to coach disabled people. It is assumed you already have the necessary sport-specific coaching knowledge and skills and are now seeking some additional knowledge and confidence. If you already adopt a coaching philosophy that focuses on building on the strengths and abilities of each individual, you will have no difficulty in meeting this new challenge. The resource will give you the necessary information and provide activities to help you apply everything to your sport and your own coaching.

Having worked through the resource, you should feel more confident and able to:

- apply and extend your existing coaching skills and experience to meet the needs of participants with a range of impairments[1]
- use appropriate terminology
- explain the benefits and problems of integrated and segregated sessions
- identify appropriate safety and medical considerations
- establish basic communication skills for coaching disabled people
- plan a coaching session for disabled participants.

If you have already attended the **scUK** workshop *How to Coach Disabled People in Sport* (formerly *Working with Disabled Sportspeople*), this will be an advantage – you will already have some awareness of types of impairments, effective communication and ways to adapt your coaching. You are also strongly encouraged to attend the workshop that accompanies this resource[2]. If you have already coached disabled people, you will be encouraged to use this experience as you work through the activities in the resource.

In this first Chapter, you will be encouraged to consider why disabled people choose to take part in sport in general and what skills and qualities coaches need to develop to work with disabled people.

1 An impairment is a temporary or permanent loss of use of a faculty or part of the body.
2 For further details, contact **sports coach UK**.

1.1 Why Sport?

Before addressing issues about how to coach, it will be useful to stop and consider:

- why disabled people become involved in sport
- what makes a good coach, and in particular, a good coach of disabled people.

The first activity encourages you to do this.

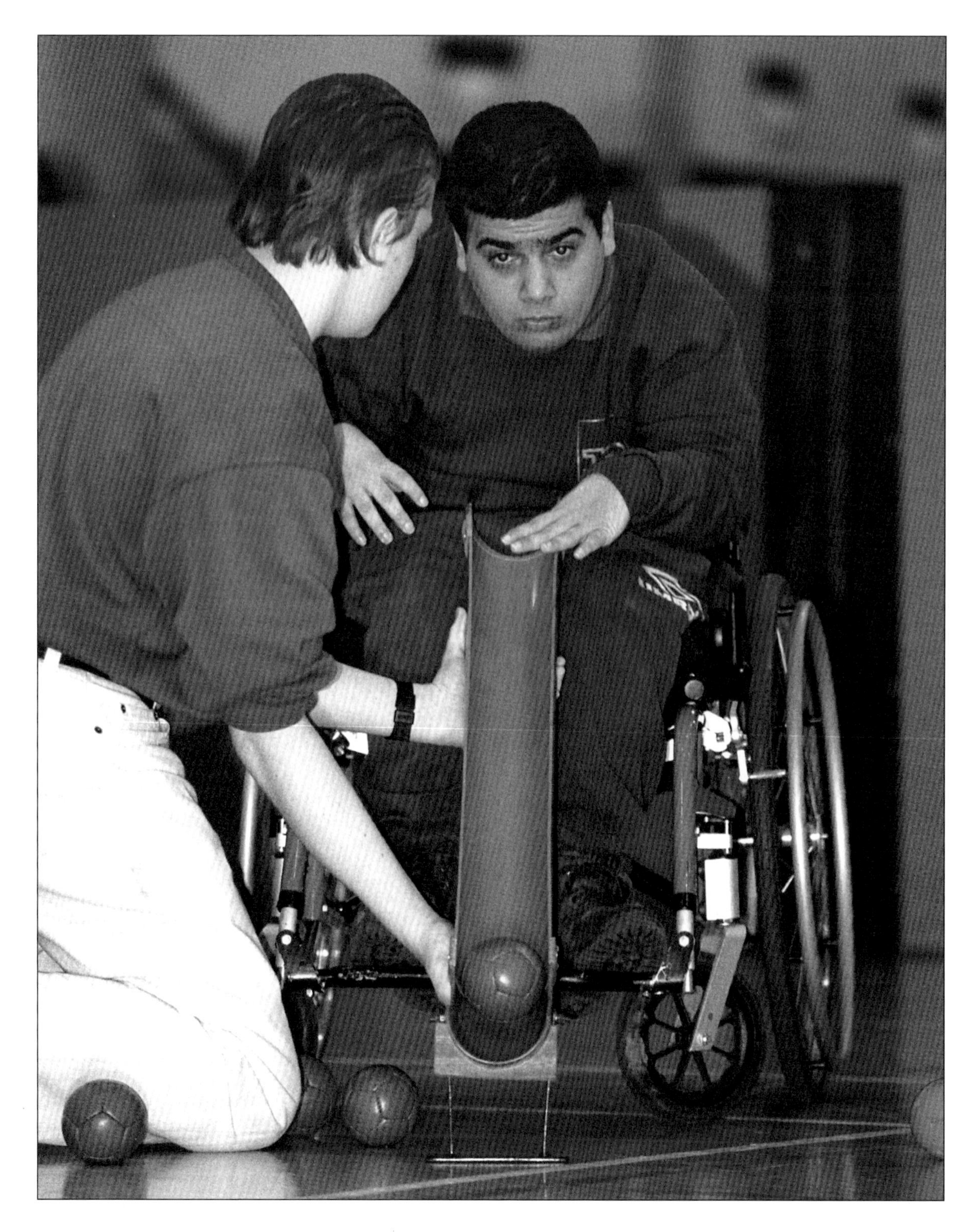

ACTIVITY 1

1. In the top left-hand box of the table below, list the reasons that non-disabled people take part in sport (you may wish to think of the people you coach).
2. In the top right-hand box, list the reasons why you think disabled people take part in sport.
3. In the lower two boxes, suggest any further benefits sport might offer these individuals (eg weight loss and improved health).
4. Note any observations:

	Non-disabled People	Disabled People
Reasons		
Benefits		
Notes		

Now turn over.

1/2 *You probably found you listed the same in each of the top boxes, because the reasons why disabled people take part in sport are the same and just as wide ranging as for non-disabled people. You may have listed reasons such as:*

- *to improve fitness*
- *to develop new skills*
- *to achieve in competition and perhaps gain recognition*
- *to make friends*
- *to experience a personal challenge*
- *to experience the thrill of competition*
- *for enjoyment.*

3 *You may also have recognised that sport can offer individuals a great deal more than simply an opportunity for participation, friendship, enjoyment and success. It can develop other skills that will enhance many areas of daily life. For example, improving confidence and self-esteem, learning how to take responsibility, handle pressure and stress, and cope with disappointments and setbacks as well as success. These are valuable skills for all people. They will be particularly important for disabled people who may gain greater independence as a result of increased fitness and mobility gained through participation in sport.*

How can the coach help people gain the potential benefits of sport? What skills and qualities does the coach need? Try Activity 2.

ACTIVITY 2

1 In the left-hand column, list the skills and qualities you feel a good coach needs:

2 In the right-hand column, list the additional skills and qualities you feel you would need to coach disabled people. You may find this a bit difficult at this stage but if you try it again after you have completed the resource, you will feel more confident in your answers.

Skills/Qualities of a Good Coach	Additional Skills/Qualities

Now turn over.

1 *Coaches, just like the individuals they coach, are all different – they have different qualities, bring different skills and experiences and coach in different ways. However, you may have been able to identify some skills and qualities you feel are very important, such as the ability to:*

- *communicate effectively – to ask questions, give and receive information, provide feedback*
- *plan and organise sessions and programmes to meet the needs of participants*
- *analyse and evaluate performance to assess and direct progress*
- *create a safe environment*
- *be open minded in developing coaching skills and knowledge*[1]

2 *In addition, in the right-hand column, you may have included:*

- *an in-depth knowledge of the individuals you are coaching*
- *a broad knowledge of an individual participant's impairment*
- *information regarding specialised equipment and adapted rules*
- *a knowledge of the relevant safety and medical implications of working with specific impairment groups.*

You have probably realised the answers you have given are very similar (or even the same) whether or not you are considering disabled participants. All coaching is about helping people to be better – better at sport and better in life in general. It is about identifying the needs of each individual and helping everyone to achieve their aspirations. Coaching disabled people is no different and the rest of the resource will continue to reinforce this point.

1.2 Terminology

Terminology can create problems. What is acceptable? How should you refer to a disability or a disabled person? What do disabled people prefer? Disabled people may have an individual, personal way of referring to their own disability.

Some definitions of disability have been based on a **medical model** (ie generalisations based on the medical condition such as everyone with Down's syndrome is overweight[2]). However, these generalisations have largely been rejected by disabled people as they focus on what disabled people **cannot** do, rather on what they can do. The **social model** of disability points out that the environment, social systems and people's attitudes are in fact what disable people. It is better to think about what disabled people can do and not about any medical label. Think also about what you do so that you can avoid disabling people by the way you coach. This will enable you to provide a positive, welcoming coaching environment.

1 For further information, read the **scUK** handbook *The Successful Coach: Guidelines for Coaching Practice* (available from Coachwise 1st4sport, Tel: 0113-201 5555).

2 Down's syndrome is congenital and caused by chromosome abnormality. For further information, see Appendix A.

Be careful with terminology. If you feel uncomfortable with a term, discuss it with the individual, but never assume what is acceptable to one person is acceptable to another, even if they have similar impairments.

1.3 Recap and Action Plan

The activities and advice in this chapter are intended to increase your interest, enthusiasm and confidence to coach disabled people. The next chapter will continue to build your confidence and knowledge.

ACTION PLAN

If you want to coach disabled people, you need to get to know them as people who enjoy sport. If you already coach disabled people, this action plan will be easy. If you do not, you will need to find one or more disabled people actively involved in sport – observe, speak to them and find out what sport means to them; talk about sport in general and your sport in particular with them. If you have difficulty in locating people, contact the English Federation of Disability Sport (EFDS). Contact details are available in Appendix E.

Make a note of your observations and feelings:

Notes:

CHAPTER 2
Providing Opportunities in Sport

2.0 What's In It For You?

This chapter examines appropriate terminology. It also identifies the different opportunities that can be made available for disabled people to participate and develop in sport. It then addresses some of the factors you would need to take into consideration when you provide these different opportunities.

By the end of this chapter, you should be able to:

- explain the Inclusion Spectrum
- describe how to adapt and modify your sport to suit the needs of disabled participants
- examine the benefits and problems of integrated and segregated sessions for different disability groups
- explain how inclusion offers more than integration.

2.1 The Inclusion Spectrum

There have been many attempts to produce a model that can help disabled people to be involved in sports activities that suit them as individuals. The Inclusion Spectrum is an activity-based model that can contribute to the inclusion of disabled participants into sports sessions. It focuses on ability rather than disability and is a good example of the application of the social model of disability, described in the previous chapter.

The Inclusion Spectrum consists of five approaches to the delivery of physical activity programmes, ranging from totally segregated to fully open activities. Each approach aims to encourage and empower disabled and non-disabled people, in order to enhance the quality of their involvement.

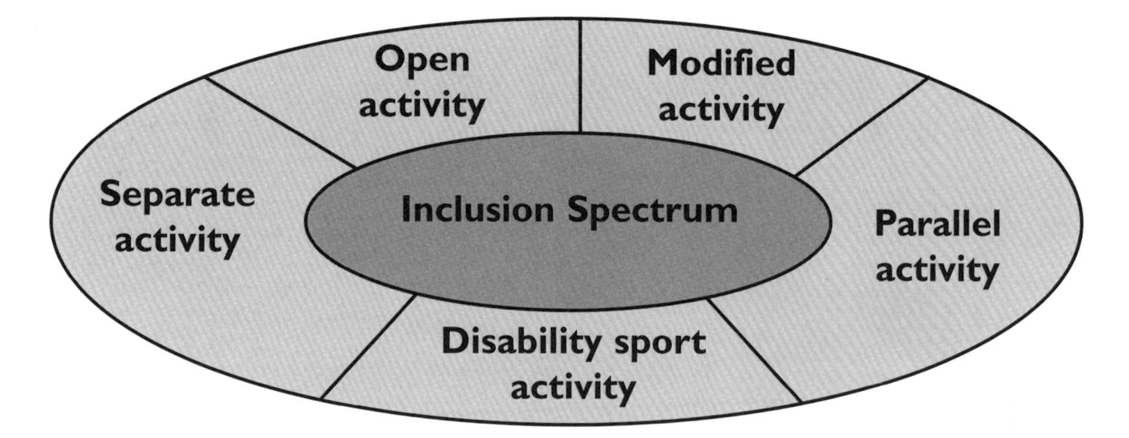

Figure 1: The Inclusion Spectrum

Reproduced with the kind permission of the English Federation of Disability Sport

Open activities

In open activities everyone does the same thing, without adaptation or modification, regardless of impairment. For example, deaf athletes doing exactly the same training schedule as hearing athletes during a track or field session.

Modified activities

In modified activities everyone does the same task but with changes to rules, areas or equipment. For example, in tennis allowing people with mobility difficulties an extra bounce before having to return the ball.

Parallel activities

In parallel activities, everyone participates in the same type of activity, but different groups participate in different ways and at different levels. Participants can be grouped according to skill, fitness or the way in which they play the game.

For example, a group of participants can be split into three smaller groups for a ball passing game such as netball. The rules, equipment and playing area can be different in all three groups to suit the requirements of the group that is playing.

Disability sport activities

In these activities a group of non-disabled participants take part in an activity that has a disability sport focus, this is reverse integration. For example, non-disabled players playing a game of basketball that has been adapted and modified to meet the needs and abilities of the disabled players in the group.

Separate activity

These are activities in which disabled participants play separately, either as individuals or in teams. This could happen, for example, when a group of disabled players practice together as a team preparing for a volleyball or tennis competition that has adapted rules to suit the needs and abilities of the individuals playing.

2.2 Adapting and Modifying Activities

Disabled people can be involved in sport in various ways but in order for this involvement to be successful, it may be necessary to adapt and modify activities such as warm ups and small sided games. Activities can be adapted and modified to suit the abilities and needs of participants by altering the equipment and the rules. Some participants may require further modifications to activities. An effective coach should be able to do this while at the same time ensuring the safety aspect of the game.

Try Activity 3 below:

ACTIVITY 3

List the ways in which your sport can be adapted to suit the needs and abilities of participants. Think of the equipment and rules. The first point has been filled in to help you.

Equipment

- use smaller/larger implements

Now turn over.

You could have come up with the following:

Equipment

- *use a smaller/larger size ball*
- *use different coloured cones/balls/implements – to contrast with background*
- *use a ball with a bell in or a with a different texture*
- *use lighter throwing implements*
- *use brightly coloured bibs*
- *mark out key areas in bright/fluorescent colours (eg perimeter of vaulting boxes, boundaries of a track, outside limits of working area, target areas).*

Rules

- *alter the size of the working/playing area or target area*
- *alter the number of participants sharing the working area*
- *use zoned playing areas*
- *simplify the scoring system*
- *vary the speed at which the participants can move*
- *rotate roles*
- *introduce safe zones where a player cannot be marked or tackled*
- *don't swap ends at half time to avoid confusion*
- *alter the tackling and passing rules*
- *alter time/speed restrictions*
- *allow guidance/direction from coach*
- *generally avoid being overly technical in officiating – allow greater scope for participants.*

The activity can be adapted and modified in many different ways. There are further opportunities to practise adapting and modifying activities in Chapter 4. It is important to remember safety, which is discussed in more detail in Chapter 3. It is also important to remember that if competition is involved between teams, the adapted and modified game has to be the same for everyone and understood by everyone involved.

2.3 Segregation, Integration and Inclusion

Activity 3 will have given you information about the various ways in which sport can be adapted to suit the needs of disabled players. However, it is also important to consider the views of those people involved in sport, especially the disabled players themselves.

For example, some disabled individuals may prefer to train and compete only with other disabled participants; others may prefer to be fully integrated. You may have to weigh up a number of other issues such as the:

- views of coaches – their ability and willingness to adapt and organise sessions appropriately (eg in relation to the inclusion continuum)
- views of non-disabled participants – they may feel they are not getting sufficient attention or their training needs are not being fully met if programmes in which disabled and non-disabled people participate together have not been structured effectively
- views of others – such as parents and helpers who may question the appropriateness of a disabled person participating in the session with non-disabled peers for a number of reasons including safety issues.

You also need to recognise there are many forms and degrees of **integration**. In some cases, it can mean playing together, sharing a facility, joint membership of a club, events for disabled people in governing body championships, joint squad training or the recruitment of disabled people as staff, committee members, officials and coaches.

Inclusion means that all players can have an opportunity to participate in sport at a suitable level with appropriate support. Disabled people can often be integrated but not necessarily included. For example, a child with restricted mobility may be integrated into a games session with non-disabled peers by being given the role of goalkeeper. For this child to be really included fully in the session, he should be given the opportunity to change roles, as should all non-disabled children when developing their games skills.

Players with disabilities and their coaches can work together in a positive way to adapt rules and equipment to accommodate their needs.

2.4 Role of the Coach

In order to provide sports opportunities for disabled players, it is your responsibility to become as familiar as possible with their individual needs and the ways in which the sport can be adapted to suit individual needs and abilities. This can be achieved by making contact with the appropriate disability sports organisation, the English Federation of Disability Sport (EFDS), the sport's National Governing Body (NGB) and, of course, by talking to the participants themselves. This will also help you become familiar with any safety requirements associated with the individual's impairment. This area is covered in greater detail in Chapter 3 and Appendix B.

Planning for success in competition and training will be motivating for you as well as your participants. If it is not possible for the player to measure success by winning a competition, set achievable goals in training by which success can be measured. By liaising with local and regional clubs and associations, you may be able to find further opportunities for competition within existing structures. If there are no opportunities available, you may be able to introduce competition for disabled players as part of existing structures.

You may be able to identify other roles for coaches to play in providing opportunities for disabled people who want to participate in your sport. These are probably similar, if not identical to those needed to work with non-disabled players. The National Disability Sports Organisations (NDSOs), sport-specific NGBs and other agencies mentioned in Appendix E will be able to offer support and guidance if required. You will also gain further help through attendance at the workshop.

2.5 Recap and Action Plan

The information in this chapter should give you an idea of the range of opportunities you can provide for disabled participants. You may have realised that it is often easier to provide coaching opportunities for individuals than to identify appropriate opportunities for competition. The next chapter looks in more detail at how you can adapt your coaching skills to meet the specific needs of disabled people who want to participate and develop in your sport.

ACTION PLAN

In the first chapter, you were encouraged to communicate with disabled people. In this activity, you are asked to find someone who already coaches disabled people, preferably in your sport. If you have difficulty, contact your NGB, the EFDS or appropriate NDSO. Contact details are to be found in Appendix E.

Find out from the coach:

- why he/she coaches disabled people:
- how he/she got started:
- what difficulties he/she has encountered:
- what satisfaction and enjoyment he/she gains:

Start to think about the people you might coach and make some notes to help you get started. For example, you may have a special interest in coaching individuals with a particular impairment. You may already know someone or be coaching a disabled person, or you may simply want to make your sport available to as many people as possible.

CHAPTER 3
Safety and Health Conditions

3.0 What's In It For You?

An awareness of safety is paramount in all coaching sessions and competitions, irrespective of whether there are disabled or non-disabled players participating. Similarly, all coaches need to be aware of any personal issues participants may have that may influence what is included in the session or how it is managed.

This chapter contains basic information for coaches about how to provide safe sport for all participants. You will be encouraged to consider the:

- same safety and personal factors you would assess for non-disabled participants
- importance of treating each player as a unique individual – as you should in all coaching situations.

There may seem to be a lot of new and perhaps rather technical or medical information in this chapter. Don't worry – you will have plenty of opportunities to return to this chapter later in the resource and start to use the information. In this way, it will start to have some real meaning in your coaching. Whatever your experience in working with disabled people, by the end of this chapter you should be able to:

- reflect on your current practice with regard to safety and personal factors and identify the key factors
- adapt your coaching practice to work effectively and safely with disabled participants.

In subsequent chapters, you will have the opportunity to put this knowledge into practice as you design and organise coaching sessions and plan for competitions.

3.1 General Considerations

The first activity in the resource provided an opportunity for reflection as well as perhaps a reminder about good coaching practice. The next one asks you to consider how you ensure safety in your current coaching situation.

ACTIVITY 4

1 In the left-hand column, list the safety factors you would consider when coaching non-disabled players.

2 In the right-hand column, add any additional factors or modifications that you believe would be important when working with disabled people (you may choose to do this for one particular group of disabled participants or generally).

General Safety Factors	Additional Factors

Now turn over.

Compare your answers with the following list regarding general safety factors:

- *Knowledge of players with, for example, epilepsy*[1]*, asthma, diabetes, anaemia, hay fever and how they manage their health.*
- *Factors relating to conditioning, new or old injuries and fatigue, so you can recognise their effect when a player is training.*
- *Number of people using a venue and the activities they are doing.*
- *Lighting and acoustics.*
- *Floor surfaces, steps and ramps.*
- *The weather and temperature, the need for fluid replacement.*
- *Location of first aid equipment.*
- *Specific hazards and safety precautions associated with your sport (eg organising a throwing session in athletics).*
- *Evacuation procedures due to emergencies (eg for fire).*

There are additional factors to consider when working with disabled participants to ensure a safe environment and coaching practice. These are explained in the next chapter so you can check your answers as you read. Remember, disabled people will be well aware of their own individual safety and personal needs. However, each person will have individual ways of dealing with personal and safety considerations.

Other factors you might need to consider include the possibility that some disabled participants may:

- *tire more quickly and so need shorter work intervals with longer rests*
- *find it harder to concentrate*
- *experience poor balance and co-ordination and so may be prone to injuries from falling, dropping objects or knocking against things*
- *need extra safety considerations for emergency evacuation as well as for access (eg there should be visual warnings as well as auditory ones for fire or bomb warnings).*

Although the disabled participants will probably not need to be told how to look after themselves, it is important for coaches to understand their needs and provide for them during training and competition.

1 Epilepsy is a tendency to have recurrent seizures due to an altered chemical state within the brain.

3.2 Specific Considerations

In this section, you will find some specific considerations pertinent to particular types of impairment. As outlined earlier, some disabled individuals may be able to participate effectively without any adaptation to rules, equipment or techniques. However, for other disabled participants, it may not be appropriate for them to participate in the full version of your sport. Such individuals may be able to participate in an adapted version of the sport such as Tag or New Image Rugby, short tennis, Unihoc or Kwik cricket.

Participants with a learning disability

As a coach, you should ensure your players understand the specific safety rules associated with your sport. Situations that appear to be an obvious danger may not be perceived as such by some individuals with a learning disability. Accidents may occur due to the lack of awareness of the imminent danger of a situation or the inability to respond appropriately and swiftly if given an instruction. Some players may have relatively poor self-care skills and will need guidance (from you or assistants) in areas such as:

- appropriate clothing. Is an outfit too hot or too cold? Does footwear fit adequately? Is an outfit suitable for the sport?
- avoidance of sunburn, exhaustion and dehydration. They may need to be reminded frequently to drink or use sun barrier creams (be aware – some medication can make skin more sensitive to the sun).

However, it is important to support the individual to be as independent as possible in such situations. Participants with a learning disability are also more likely than their non-disabled peers to have convulsive disorders such as epilepsy or asthma (see Appendix B). If a player has epilepsy or asthma, it is important to understand how it is dealt with on an individual level as this can differ from one person to another.

Other safety issues to be aware of:

- Some individuals may have low or high pain thresholds.
- Some participants may not react to certain situations as you think they will – expect the unexpected.
- If additional assistance is required, ensure those assisting understand what is expected of them, from both the participant and you as a coach.

It is important to discuss the safety issues involved, not only with the disabled person but also with other non-disabled participants involved in the programme. For example, in hockey, rugby, football or basketball, it may be that some players should never be tackled while in possession of the ball, so adopt the wearing of different coloured shorts or bibs to indicate this to other players.

Amputee participants

Some amputee players use a **prosthesis**[1]. An everyday prosthesis, as the name suggests, is not designed to withstand the pressures of training and competition, so players should be advised to see a prosthetist to have a sports modified prosthesis. Modern technology and materials ensure that a prosthesis is immensely strong and extremely light. Artificial knee joints have built in computers and artificial feet are made from carbon fibre to allow the individual to move in a similar way to that of a natural limb or joint. If a prosthesis fails (ie splits or breaks) it could cause an injury so coaches need to ensure the participant:

- checks that the prosthesis is suitable for the sport
- regularly checks the prosthesis for signs of wear
- is aware that it may take some time to get used to a new prosthesis
- responds to complaints of soreness in the lower back, by referring to the prosthetist to check length and weight[2].

Amputee players have greater difficulty **regulating body temperature** because the ratio of surface area to body volume is different and could result in overheating. Coaches must therefore ensure players wear suitable clothing and ample opportunities are provided for rehydration and recovery.

It is important to take good care of the **stump** – the stump sock (worn over the stump to protect it) needs to be changed regularly as it can produce soreness or become slippery if covered in sweat. If the stump becomes blistered, the player will miss out on training or competition. The stump should be checked regularly by the player and any breaks of skin treated to avoid infection and allow healing. It may be necessary to organise alternative training to allow the stump to heal. If the prosthesis is rubbing the stump, refer the player to the prosthetist.

Participants with cerebral palsy

Cerebral palsy is not a disease or illness. It is a brain lesion that is non-progressive and causes variable impairment of the coordination, tone and strength of muscle action impacting on postures and movement. The degree of impairment between individuals with cerebral palsy varies considerably according to the severity and site of the brain damage. No two people with cerebral palsy are alike because the brain damage that causes the condition can evolve differently in each individual. You may not be very familiar with this condition, so it may help to meet the individual first before considering the particular safety issues of which you need to be aware.

1 Artificial replacement for a limb of the body.

2 Refer to the British Amputee and Les Autres Sports Association (BALASA) for advice from a prosthetist with specific knowledge of sport.

Participants with cerebral palsy may be ambulant[1] or use wheelchairs for mobility (see Appendix A for more information). Players may be prone to **accidents and injuries** because they have problems with balance and co-ordination. The types of injuries that people with cerebral palsy may acquire will depend on the nature of the sport and the degree of their impairment. For example, ambulant basketball players will have different considerations (their legs) from players using wheelchairs, who will need to consider their upper body requirements.

Individuals with cerebral palsy may also more frequently experience **dehydration, muscle cramps** and **exhaustion**. Coaches and assistants therefore need to take extra precautions in hot weather and during hard training sessions, by giving opportunities for rest and to take on liquids. Similarly, if there is poor motor efficiency, players will be more prone to exhaustion after intense effort. As a coach you should be aware of this and monitor drills and training schedules accordingly.

Participants with a visual impairment

When coaching visually impaired participants, it is useful to remember the following basic points with regard to safety:

- Do not leave equipment lying on the floor and always leave it in the same place each session so people know where it is.
- Allow participants time to orientate themselves in a venue and pinpoint any potential dangers such as slippery areas, doorways and obstacles.
- Be aware of any changes in the environment that could cause an injury, such as open doors, cupboards, windows, discarded kit or even someone walking into an open space unannounced.

Some specific medical conditions need extra considerations:

- Individuals with a **detached retina**[2] could be at risk of further detachment if they experience blows to the head.
- Participants with **glaucoma**[3] should gain medical advice regarding activities which require exertion.

Participants with a hearing impairment

Communication difficulties can result in accidents. Coaches must give sufficient time to ensure that participants with hearing impairments fully understand safety regulations and procedures. It is useful if venues have a visual stimulus as well as a fire alarm and staff are aware that individuals who have a hearing impairment (or a visual impairment) are in the venue. Some people will wear hearing aids and you will need to determine when it is safer to wear them or leave them off (eg when swimming).

1 Non-wheelchair users.

2 This involves the detachment of the light sensitive layer at the back of the eye on which the incoming light rays are focused.

3 This occurs when there is an abnormally high amount of fluid in the eyeball which exerts pressure onto the retina and the optic nerve. This can eventually lead to blindness.

Participants who use wheelchairs

Wheelchair sports such as basketball, tennis and rugby are normally played by people with a lower limb impairment such as paraplegia[1]. There may be some people who use wheelchairs who want to experience the wheelchair version of a sport but may not necessarily be paraplegic.

The following basic points apply to individuals who have paraplegia and tetraplegia. You will find some additional points that refer specifically to performers with tetraplegia:

- Paralysis affects the body's ability to perspire below the site of the lesion, so **overheating** may occur. Therefore, participants should be encouraged to drink regularly, seek shade between drills or events when training, wear light clothing and use spray bottles to cool off. Individuals with tetraplegia are even more susceptible to temperature regulation problems.
- Some people may have relatively poor **circulation** so need to change their sitting position regularly to encourage blood flow. Poor circulation may also cause dizziness. As circulation is even poorer in participants with tetraplegia, dizzy spells may be more frequent. An elasticated corset worn around the upper stomach and lower rib cage can help to reduce dizziness as can breathing deeply and changing posture.
- Wheelchair users are prone to **pressure sores** because of poor circulation and movement restrictions. They should be encouraged to watch out for signs of pressure sores (eg redness, inflammation, skin breaking down) and take preventative care (eg massage, change of position, medical advice). Pressure sores take longer to heal because of poor circulation and could affect a player's training and competition schedule.

As a coach, you should be aware that some wheelchair users use special appliances or procedures to compensate for loss of **bowel or bladder control**. Usually, the only requirement for individuals is privacy and adequate facilities for carrying out necessary personal procedures. However, you should be aware that some personal procedures will need to be continued during a training programme or competition so these needs must be accommodated.

Occasionally, accidents occur because individuals are unable to feel sensation in their limbs. For example, hand blistering as a result of pushing, and cuts and scrapes from wheels can usually be avoided through adequate taping of the fingers and the use of padded gloves.

Participants with tetraplegia may have decreased breathing efficiency because the diaphragm muscle may be the only respiratory muscle that remains in working order. This sometimes affects the ability to cough and clear the airway, so infections are more likely to occur. Exercise can improve the development of muscles in the neck that can improve breathing efficiency. If a chest or breathing difficulty is noticed, the player should always seek medical advice.

1 Paraplegia refers to paralysis of the lower part of the body. For more information see Appendix B.

Players with tetraplegia may suffer from automatic dysreflexia[1], which can result in high blood pressure, sweating, chills and headaches. If a person is unable to feel there is something wrong because of lack of sensation, these reactions will be the first indication of a problem elsewhere in the body. It is important to try to find the cause of the reaction by ensuring that bladders are able to empty freely and there are no obvious sites of injury. If this does not help the participant recover, seek immediate medical advice.

Participants with spina bifida

The same considerations should be taken into account as for individuals with paraplegia. However, if the participant has hydrocephalus[2] she may have a shunt[3] fitted. It is important to take care not to displace the shunt when lifting or transferring her. If a participant complains of headaches, nausea and dizziness, it is wise to seek medical advice to ensure the shunt is working properly.

3.3 Recap and Action Plan

The information in this chapter is intended as a guide to some of the safety and personal/medical issues coaches need to consider. It is always preferable to discuss specific requirements with individuals to ensure their needs are understood. If you require more information on any of the contents of this chapter, you are recommended to contact the appropriate NDSO or the relevant disability organisation (addresses in Appendix E).

1 Automatic dysreflexia or hyperflexia is a reaction of parts of the body to various stimuli that are outside conscious control. For example, an over extended bladder or a limb that has been kept in a painful position can trigger a reaction.

2 Hydrocephalus is an accumulation of cerebrospinal fluid in the brain that makes it swell. For more information see Appendix A.

3 Shunts are inserted into the cranium to remove excess cerebrospinal fluid. For more information see Appendix A.

ACTION PLAN

If you already know a disabled participant, go back and read again all the safety and health issues regarding his specific impairment. If you do not yet know a disabled participant, concentrate on becoming familiar with the safety and health issues regarding the disabled person or people you are most likely to work with. Make a note of all the factors with which you should be particularly concerned but remember that each person is different, even if they have the same impairment. Make full use of Appendices A and B:

Individual/disability group:

Impairment:

Key factors to consider:

•

•

CHAPTER 4

Implications for Coaching

4.0 What's In It For You?

This chapter will help you identify how you can adapt your coaching to meet the needs of people with different impairments. Again, it is important to emphasise these pointers are made in very general terms and the more familiar a coach becomes with an individual, the easier it should be to establish successful coaching strategies.

By the end of the chapter you should be able to:

- describe how to adapt your communication skills and coaching style to meet the needs of individual participants
- plan coaching sessions for players in an integrated setting and on an individual basis
- identify key points for coaching people with learning disabilities, visual or hearing impairments, physical disabilities and/or a combination of these.

4.1 Communication and Coaching Style

A key element of successful coaching is effective communication – this means giving and receiving information. Both are equally important. How you communicate and the way you build relationships with your participants will determine, to a large extent, how effective your coaching will be. Most coaches do a lot of telling and showing, good coaches also do plenty of questioning and listening. You may find there are additional challenges to how you coach and the way you communicate when coaching disabled players. The **scUK** workshop entitled **Coaching Methods and Communication** addresses this area in greater detail[1].

Giving information

Information can be shared in many ways – speaking is the most common but do not underestimate the impact of non-verbal communication such as gestures, expressions and even posture. The latter can be more powerful than the actual words spoken – it is suggested that 90% of information is actually conveyed non-verbally. Of course, non-verbal forms of communication can become *the* form of communication for those with hearing impairments. Most coaches are good at giving information but remember it is important to give not just relevant information but an appropriate amount and in the right way (ie in terms of tone and pitch as well as the actual words chosen and the complexity). Too much information can lead to boredom and even frustration and this may be particularly true if there are challenges to communication – for example when working with those individuals who have a learning disability, speech or hearing impairment. Whoever you coach, please remember that too much negative information can reduce self-confidence, progress and enjoyment.

1 For details of workshops in your area, telephone **sports coach UK** on 0113-274 4802, or find details on the website at www.sportscoachuk.org

Gaining information

Compared with information-giving skills, coaches often tend to be relatively poor at asking good questions and really listening to what individuals have to say. Coaches can learn a great deal about their participants, their strengths, weaknesses, hopes and fears, if they listen to them and ask questions.

The use of open questions (ie those which demand a response other than simply 'yes' or 'no') is important in any coaching environment but it is particularly valuable when coaching disabled people – they all have very individual needs and goals. It is too easy to make assumptions about what they want or what they can and cannot do. Always ask so you really get to know each participant as an individual and build a good relationship with her.

Again coaches working with disabled players may need to become particularly skilled at a variety of different methods of communication – different ways of giving information by telling, showing and guiding and different ways of gaining information by listening, watching and asking. The next sections point out some of the special skills required. It is important however to emphasise these pointers are made in very general terms and the more familiar a coach becomes with an individual, the easier it will be to establish successful communication strategies.

Communicating with participants who have a learning disability

The following points should help you communicate effectively with players with learning disabilities (remember not to make assumptions about an individual's communication requirements):

- Speak to the individual, not to the person accompanying them.
- Establish the extent to which instructions and directions are understood.
- Use simple, brief, concise language, without being patronising.
- Refer to participants according to their chronological age and encourage other players, officials and supporters to use age-appropriate and sports-specific terminology (eg 'you paced yourself well' rather than 'good boy').
- Be aware that not every participant will understand the jargon and technical terms associated with your sport.
- Some people with learning disabilities may use a signing system to support speech called Makaton. These individuals are not necessarily deaf or have no speech, but may be unable to communicate effectively by oral methods alone. For more information on Makaton, use the contact details in Appendix E.
- Some participants may need more time to be able to say something; be patient and don't finish off their sentences.
- You may have difficulty understanding some individuals initially; the better you know them, the easier this should become.
- Ask participants to repeat what they have said if you have not understood them. You can also ask questions to which the answer is either 'yes' or 'no' to establish whether or not you have understood a player.
- Be aware that an individual's ability to communicate by speech, or their ability to read something, may not reflect their level of understanding.

If you need to communicate in writing with players with learning disabilities, establish the most appropriate method for each individual. This may mean:

- using short sentences without jargon or long and complicated words
- supporting words with diagrams, photographs or pictures
- using larger print and a different typeface
- copying what you have written to a parent or friend – making sure you ask the individual first whom they want to share the information with
- using symbols such as Makaton or Bliss.

Communicating with participants with visual impairments

The next activity will help you think through the challenges you may face when working with visually impaired performers.

ACTIVITY 5

In the box below, list what you think you would need to consider when coaching participants with a visual impairment.

Participants with a visual impairment

Now turn over.

Participants with a visual impairment can usually be coached in a similar way to their sighted peers. As a coach, you need sound sport-specific knowledge and the ability to communicate this knowledge effectively to the individuals. However, you may have listed the following in your answer:

- *Always address the player by name and state your own name.*
- *Do not walk away from the player without telling him.*
- *You may need to use touch but always ask first as any physical contact needs to be sensitive and appropriate.*
- *Use key words what you are trying to say and avoid long complicated.*
- *Be logical and sequential when presenting information.*
- *Ensure verbal instructions are concise and accurate. If visually impaired participants do not understand instructions, they may not be able to copy sighted players.*
- *Be aware of the influence of environmental factors that can influence how you communicate. For example:*
  - *amount of available light*
  - *changes in light (eg cloud cover)*
  - *type of light (eg sun, fluorescent lights, floodlights)*
  - *positioning of individuals and/or the coach in relation to the light source*
  - *level of background noise (eg echo or reverberation, ventilation fans).*

Establish with players how these can affect communication during coaching sessions and competition.

If a visually impaired person needs guidance, it may be useful initially to enlist the help of family and friends to assist in coaching sessions; they would be more familiar with guiding the individual. Eventually, it may be that sighted participants in the coaching session would be able to assist.

It is the decision of the coach and the participant, whether or not it is safe or appropriate to be coached in your sport. For specific information on coaching people with visual impairments, you are recommended to contact British Blind Sport (contact details are available in Appendix E).

Communicating with participants with hearing impairments

Communicating with participants who are deaf or hard of hearing may create other challenges. The next activity will help you think through the challenges you may face when working with hearing impaired people.

ACTIVITY 6

In the box below, list what you think you would need to consider when coaching participants who have hearing impairments.

Participants with a hearing impairment

Now turn over.

As with all participants, it is beneficial to take time to get to know participants with hearing impairments to establish the most appropriate means of communication. It may be that an individual has residual hearing and uses a hearing aid, making it possible to communicate orally with the participant. However, the individual will also need to see your mouth so there is the opportunity to lip-read. This will reinforce what you are saying. For more information on hearing impairments, see Appendix A. The sort of factors you may have listed include the following:

- *Ensure your face is well-lit. For example if out-of-doors, face the sun as this will assist the player who may be lip-reading or reading signs. If inside, ensure your face is lit from the front so that your mouth can easily be seen.*
- *Face the participants at all times when speaking to them. If you turn your head, they will no longer be able to read your lips.*
- *Do not chew, shout or cover your mouth with your hand when talking – again, this will prevent lip-reading.*
- *Remember that lip-reading is not a precise way of communicating. Do not presume that if an individual can lip-read, every word will automatically be understood. Much of lip-reading is intelligent guesswork.*
- *Ensure that the coaching or competition environment is accommodating (eg no background noise to interfere with concentration).*
- *You may need to be near the person to attract attention (eg by tapping on a shoulder). Other means of attracting attention may need to be established such as flicking lights on and off or waving.*
- *Keep sentences simple and avoid unnecessary jargon. This is particularly important for individuals who have been born with a hearing loss. Language skills (written and spoken) will be based on different principles to those of standard English. It is always useful to establish the meaning of any sport-specific or technical language before you start a session.*
- *If relevant, provide written information, but do not give them the written information to read and then continue to speak as the person will be unable to lip-read or even be aware that you are speaking. Be aware that some participants may be able to read your lips even if you are standing a distance away and not talking directly to them.*
- *Develop your own simple system of signs and gestures with your participants such as 'thumbs up' for 'Yes!' or 'Good!'.*

You will subsequently be able to plan an individual programme. If an individual has to remove a hearing aid, for example in training, it is useful to establish mutually identifiable signs or gestures before it is removed. This will also help other participants such as teammates. It is important to raise your voice when the hearing aid is not being worn.

You may be approached by a hearing impaired participant who is unable to communicate orally. Again, you will have to establish the most appropriate means of communication. This may mean:

- using an interpreter who might be a parent, friend or teacher or a fully qualified individual – the Royal National Institute for the Deaf (RNID) will be able to provide you with information regarding hiring professional interpreters (address in Appendix E)
- learning to sign or finger spell – RNID will again be able to advise
- establishing mutually identifiable signs or gestures
- identifying whether or not the person can lip-read.

Deaf participants can achieve and require the same coaching expertise as hearing players. However, it is useful to appreciate that many deaf people refer to themselves as *the Deaf*. This can be associated with the fact that being deaf is a cultural issue as well as a description of an impairment group. As with first experience of any new culture, Deaf culture can be difficult for hearing people to understand and accept, and can lead to misunderstandings and frustration.

Although deaf participants can compete and be coached in the same situation as hearing individuals, they often prefer to be in situations with other deaf people. This can be for a number of reasons, including cultural similarities and communication issues. As a coach, it is important to respect the person's **choice** and appreciate the strong cultural identity of some deaf people.

Communicating with participants who use wheelchairs

The following information may be useful if you are coaching individuals who use wheelchairs:

- Address the individual, not the person who may accompany them.
- Talk to the person face to face and at eye level. Either sit down or kneel but be in a comfortable position if you intend to hold a long conversation.
- Talk to the participant with the sun or light shining on your face to illuminate it.

Establish the level of understanding of the individual by asking questions or asking for a demonstration.

The last two points are, of course, important coaching points for all participants.

Communicating with participants with cerebral palsy

The following information may be useful if you are coaching individuals who have cerebral palsy:

- Individuals with cerebral palsy may have speech impairment. This should not automatically be associated with the individual having a learning disability (although some individuals may have).
- Individual players may have devised individual means of communication. It is useful to spend time getting to know the player in order to learn and understand these means of communication.

Additional information about cerebral palsy can be found in Appendix A.

4.2 Planning and Organising Sessions and Programmes

Having established a few guidelines about safety and health issues, and how to improve your ability to communicate effectively with disabled people, next you need to consider what to coach. Is the session or programme planning any different? Do you need to adapt the content of your coaching sessions, as well as the way you communicate when coaching?

All the general principles of how to establish goals and plan and organise coaching sessions are equally applicable when coaching your sport to disabled people[1]. In addition, you will need to think carefully about the following:

- Are additional safety checks necessary?
- The need for individualised goals may be even more important.
- How to adapt the way you deliver and organise the session to accommodate everyone.
- The length, intensity and frequency of sessions as well as the drills or activities within each session. For example, some disabled participants tire more quickly, others need regular rests to avoid pressure sores, some have difficulty regulating temperature and need to rehydrate more frequently.
- The structure and sequencing of sessions. You may need to:
  - be creative in finding a variety of ways to explain or develop a particular skill
  - adapt drills and warm-ups to accommodate the needs of particular individuals
  - modify equipment and adapt rules to maximise opportunities for participation and achievement.

It is also useful to remember to take into consideration the experience of the participants. It may be that you are introducing your sport for the first time, so even though the players are not children you should be able to use the information contained in any continuum of skill/game progression that your sport employs (eg the modified, progressive games developed by netball, cricket and rugby). However, it is important to treat the players by their chronological age. Do not patronise them.

Other disabled individuals may have participated in your sport before acquiring their disability. In these circumstances, it is important to establish skill levels and discuss what modifications and adaptations, if any, are needed to enable the person to participate safely.

1 For further guidance, you are recommended to read Chapter 2 of the **scUK** resource *The Successful Coach*. (Available from Coachwise 1st4sport, tel: 0113-201 5555).

Some disabled individuals may never participate in the full version of the sport, because of the safety issues involved and because they may not be able to acquire a particular skill. However, they may be able to play an adapted version of the sport.

In addition to these general pointers, there are specific factors to consider when coaching people with different types of disability – some of these are highlighted on the following pages.

Coaching players with a learning disability

A learning disability is where an individual's central nervous system (CNS – the brain and spinal column) does not develop as fast or as fully as a person without a learning disability. This can be for several reasons, for example, because of an accident or as the result of contracting an infection.

Participants with a learning disability will have a wide range of abilities. Never make assumptions about what they can and cannot do as each participant is an individual with her own personality and ability. Some people with learning disabilities may have additional impairments and health issues such as epilepsy. (More information can be found in Appendix B.)

As a coach, it is important to build upon the abilities of the players you are working with. It is therefore useful to have some knowledge of the learning disabled players before you plan an introductory coaching session. Now try the activity below.

ACTIVITY 7

In the box below, list what you would need to know about the participants to enable you to plan an appropriate introductory coaching session for people with a learning disability:

Now turn over.

You may have thought of all or some of the following:

- *level of understanding*
- *level of fitness*
- *level of coordination*
- *level of concentration and attention*
- *sport-specific skill level*
- *time taken to remember and acquire new skills*
- *appropriate means of communication (more information in Section 4.1)*
- *level of awareness of safety issues (more information in Section 3.2)*
- *ability to transfer skills*
- *personal likes and dislikes*
- *individual responses to instructions*
- *level of motivation*
- *their aspirations and desires.*

You could find out all of the above by visiting the individuals, for example in their school or club environment, and talking to them or observing them. It may be useful to organise some kind of physical activity for the participants that will enable you to observe them with limited intervention to ensure safety. In addition, as with everyone you coach, you would need to be aware of any health issues or other individual or personal needs that a participant may have.

The following points should also help you to continue to plan appropriate coaching sessions:

- Many learning disabled people will enjoy regular routines and well structured activities, although it is important to be flexible.
- A variety of activities will help to maintain concentration and attention.
- Set realistic and achievable goals.
- Keep instructions short, don't link too many instructions together but take care not to patronise the players.
- Introduce technical terms slowly so people have time to become familiar with them.
- Try not to link too many skills or movements together.
- Be aware that many participants respond best in individual or small group settings.
- Give enough time for individuals to practise the application and transference of skills to different situations.
- Try different approaches to teaching skills. For example, you could try the *whole skill* approach, where an individual is taught a skill such as catching a ball by a feeder throwing the ball to the catcher; or you could try *chaining*, where a skill is broken down into its smallest parts and the person is taught each part separately then joins them together.
- Use demonstrations; sometimes you may need to use a *hands on* approach, but do this only with the consent of the player and follow your NGB's guidelines.
- Always use positive feedback – you may need to do this more frequently for some people because of their lack of self-esteem and self-confidence. Again, be careful not to appear to patronise the player.
- Ensure the equipment being used is suitable and adequate. For example, you may need to use more cones to mark areas or different coloured balls to help people differentiate tasks.
- Give plenty of opportunities to repeat and practise.
- Be patient, consistent and tactful but ensure individuals understand the boundaries of acceptable behaviour.
- Be aware that the motor skills and physical fitness of some players may be generally poor due to lack of opportunities to participate in sporting activities or even regular day-to-day exercise.
- Avoid using abstract models.
- Enable simple decision making.
- Avoid drills that rely heavily on numeracy and literacy skills.
- Coach by showing and copying, not telling.
- Be aware that some individuals may need more time than others for changing and showering after a session.

- Some participants may need guidance regarding appropriate clothing and footwear for training and competition.
- You may have to consider transport arrangements when planning a session.

Finally, while considering all the preceding points, don't forget to make sessions **fun** and **enjoyable**. Whoever you coach, this will always help you and the participants achieve their goals.

It is useful to remember that the cause of an individual's learning disability may also affect that person's development physically, socially and emotionally as well as cognitively. Further advice can be obtained from the UK Sports Association for People with Learning Disability (see Appendix E for contact details).

Coaching amputee participants

When coaching amputee participants you should consider the following:

- How movement is affected.
- What movement patterns are already established.
- Any poor technique that may need to be re-taught.
- Level of motivation and personal goals.
- Understanding of personal safety and any health issues.
- Whether or not the participant can be fully included in the session.
- An appropriate warm-up.
- The age of the participant.
- Which limb or part of limb is missing.
- Does the individual need any assistance.
- Whether the amputation is acquired or congenital. This may affect, for example, the length of time a participant may be able to train as some congenital amputees have less stump soreness than amputees who have lost a limb through injury.
- Whether the person has had time to adjust to the loss of a limb. Frustration at being unable to do something may lead to outbursts of anger.
- Whether specific exercises are needed to strengthen the remaining muscles, for example in above knee amputees, to ensure muscle wastage does not occur.
- Phantom pain or other sensations may appear to occur in the amputated portion of the limb. This may cause discomfort or embarrassment and participants may be reluctant, at first, to tell coaches.

It is helpful to realise that some individuals may have only recently had a leg amputated as a result of an accident or a disease so may cope with their impairment in a different way to a person who has had much longer to adjust.

If an amputee participant requires further assistance on personal safety, prosthesis and medical care, direct them to the British Amputees and Les Autres Sports Association (BALASA). Contact details are available in Appendix E.

Coaching participants who have a hearing impairment

When coaching participants who have a hearing impairment you should consider the following:

- How to communicate instructions.
- The communication needs of the individual.
- Any distractions such as noise from other people using the facilities.
- Additional safety issues such as participants needing to remove hearing aids before training.
- Whether the person understands what is required during the session.
- Whether the hearing participants understand each person's specific communication needs.

Coaching participants with cerebral palsy

It is important to remember that the specific needs of one individual participant with cerebral palsy may be totally different from another participant with cerebral palsy. Some people are able to take charge of their own personal safety and health needs, but others may require additional support because of their impairment. Sport can have many benefits for people with cerebral palsy, for example, improving muscle control, flexibility, posture, balance, coordination and cardio-respiratory efficiency, especially breathing.

There are some other considerations when coaching people with cerebral palsy:

- If the participant requires assistance to attend coaching sessions, is there an enabler (relative or friend) available who can offer support?
- Is the enabler fully aware of what is required and what is not required when supporting the individual (eg the nature of the participant's personal needs and how to assist during a coaching session if required)?
- What special equipment do you need? Information can be obtained from CP Sport (address in Appendix E).
- What level of support do you require? Consideration needs to be given to:
  - personal requirements (eg dressing, eating)
  - transport
  - support with training programmes
  - who does what.
- Do you need to consider any specific safety or health issues? (See Appendix A and B.)

It is helpful to be aware that individuals with cerebral palsy may be more likely to have epilepsy than their non-disabled peers. If an individual has epilepsy, it is useful to establish how he copes with seizures on a personal basis and what procedures you should follow (See Appendix B). Some participants may have a learning disability as well as a physical disability plus other associated impairments such as a speech impediment.

Coaching participants who use wheelchairs

You may be able to accommodate wheelchair users in your usual coaching sessions. To do this you need to consider the following:

- The accessibility of facilities.
- Whether a person requires assistance and if so, how this should be provided.
- What range of movement the individual has.
- How you might need to adapt the way you coach the skills, organise the activities or adapt the rules or equipment to make the session enjoyable and worthwhile for disabled and non-disabled participants.
- Whether the wheelchair the individual uses is the best design for your sport or should you try to find a sport-specific wheelchair for them.

Make sure that you respect a person's independence and space around the wheelchair. For example, it is generally accepted that you should not:

- move a participant when seated in their wheelchair – ask them to move
- lean on a wheelchair or hang things from it
- assume an individual needs a push or additional help, for example, when carrying a kit bag – always ask.

Coaching players with visual impairments

When coaching participants who have a visual impairment you should consider the following:

- Communication. For example, no demonstrations should be conducted from a distance.
- Different levels of spatial awareness; visually impaired participants can have difficulty adjusting from an indoor to an outdoor environment.
- Time for individuals to orientate their surroundings, including changing and toilet facilities or boundary cones in the playing area.
- Type of equipment, possibly use a brighter coloured ball or one which makes a sound when it moves.
- Noise distractions should be eliminated.
- Equipment should not be left on the floor where it may be a hazard.

The following activities should help you think about how to adapt and modify your coaching sessions to the needs of disabled participants in a variety of situations. The activities are based on the following groups in which the individuals have never played your sport before but have experienced a wide range of other sports.

Group 1

This is a group of ten people, aged 20 years and over, with severe learning disabilities, who are ambulant and reasonably fit.

Group 2

This is a group of 15 people aged 10–12 years; 14 are non-disabled and one uses a wheelchair. All participants are fit and are used to working with each other in sports activities.

Group 3

This is a group of 15 people, aged 14 years; 14 are non-disabled and one has cerebral palsy. He is ambulant but weak on his right side therefore having difficulty catching and throwing with his right hand.

Group 4

This is a group of 15 people, aged 8–9 years; 14 are non-disabled and one is an amputee who uses a prosthesis for her lower left leg.

Group 5

This is a group of 15 players, aged 12 years; one of the group has a moderate learning disability, he is clumsy and often falls over.

ACTIVITY 8

Think of how the warm up/introductory activities section of a coaching session is typically undertaken in your sport.

How would you adapt/modify the session to ensure the five groups previously described could participate? Write your answers below:

Group 1

Group 2

Group 3

Group 4

Group 5

Now turn over.

You could have come up with the following:

Group 1

- *Make sure the participants understand what is required of them, if they don't, try a simpler version of the activity.*
- *You may need to use more, or fewer working areas and have them marked more obviously.*
- *You may initially need to use more coaches or support staff, to enable the participants to succeed and become familiar with what is required of them.*
- *You may need to repeat the exercise. If this is as far as you get in one session, it doesn't matter as long as the participants are enjoying themselves and doing the activity correctly.*

Group 2

- *The session would need to be taken on a hard surface.*
- *You may need to alter the number of working areas.*
- *In a team game, the wheelchair user could be allowed to touch other players with the ball only when they are either side of him so he does not run into them.*
- *In a passing game, the wheelchair participant could carry the ball on his lap but has to pass after two pushes (or wheel revolutions – a coloured tape on the wheel helps to count these). Alternatively he may be prohibited from touching other participants with the ball but must be part of a passing sequence before anyone else can touch the rest of the group.*
- *The wheelchair participant may be able to remove the foot plates from her wheelchair, check whether this makes participating safer or more dangerous. Similarly discuss whether straps round the legs are an advantage or disadvantage (always check with the individual and an appropriate other person before doing this).*

Group 3

- *Ensure the individual has plenty of practice with his left hand.*
- *The player may find it easier to throw and catch if he turns his left side towards the person he is receiving from or throwing to.*
- *Narrow the distance the player has to cover when sending and/or receiving an object.*
- *You may need to vary the speeds at which the other participants can move if the individual with cerebral palsy is unable to contribute fully.*

Group 4

- *There may not be a need to adapt the warm up/introductory activities.*
- *If the individual cannot move as quickly as other participants (eg in a ball-tag game) it may be necessary to encourage her to pass quickly and accurately so other players can touch the rest of the group.*
- *In a team game, you may need to introduce the rule that the participant is included in each passing sequence before other players can touch the rest of the group.*

Group 5

- *There may be a need to adapt the warm up.*

ACTIVITY 9

Now consider the typical skill learning/development phase of a coaching session in your sport. How would you adapt/modify the session to ensure the five groups described previously could participate? Write your answers below:

Group 1

Group 2

Group 3

Group 4

Group 5

Now turn over.

It is difficult to provide feedback that would cover all sports. Check your responses by reading/re-reading the relevant sections in this resource and discussing your responses and any issues with disabled people and other coaches.

The preceding, hypothetical situations are inevitably artificial but they will have given you opportunities to adapt your coaching practice in the light of the information you have gained by working through this resource.

The most important way to check the effectiveness of your plans is to try running sessions and monitoring carefully what happens. Ask yourself what went well and what did not go well and may need to be adapted in the future? Remember, you will not become an expert overnight – you will need to develop your skills and experience. This will only happen as you start to coach your sport to disabled people and you can develop more rapidly by either observing a more experienced coach at work or using that coach as a sounding board to try out your ideas and help you meet the challenges as they arise.

4.3 Recap and Action Plan

You may now feel ready to take the next step – whatever that might be. Some of you will have gained new knowledge and perhaps confidence to help with the coaching you are already doing with disabled participants. Others may feel very excited and ready to accept the challenge of starting to coach – you may already know someone who is seeking coaching support or you may wish to make contact with national or local disability groups to see how you could become involved. However, some of you may feel they have neither the confidence or perhaps desire to coach disabled people – you may wish to go no further or perhaps become involved in helping other coaches from time to time. Perhaps you are still unsure. Whatever you feel is the next step for you at your particular stage of development, you may wish to try one or more of the recommended actions.

ACTION PLAN A

1 Find a coach who is working with disabled people in your local area. You can use your sport's national governing body and/or the address list in Appendix E to help you.

2 Arrange to meet with the coach before the session and find out as much as you can about:

- how long the coach has been involved in coaching disabled people and how she got started
- how long the coach has been working with these particular participants
- the goals and needs of the participants
- the main challenges the coach has had to meet
- the particular goals of the session you will go to watch – a copy of the session plan would be ideal if there is one available.

3 Observe the session and make detailed notes.

4 After the session, you may wish to spend some further time with the coach to seek answers to some of the questions you may have about the session, her approach, the participants or the way forward.

ACTION PLAN B

If it is possible, you are strongly encouraged to try to run a coaching session with disabled people and complete a very detailed evaluation of:

- what went well
- what perhaps did not work as well as you might have expected
- what you might do differently next time
- what further information or help you might need.

Try to spend some time with the participants to establish their goals and needs before you run the session – you may wish to modify some parts of the session plan. Record your evaluations and design the next coaching session based on your experiences.

Evaluations:

CONCLUSION

This resource cannot provide all the answers to every query about coaching your sport to disabled people. However, it should have given you a sound foundation of advice, knowledge and skills and some direction to additional sources of information through the appendices.

By working through this resource and completing the activities, you should have gained sufficient information to enable you to work confidently with disabled people and adapt your coaching skills accordingly. Of course, your confidence will increase as you gain more experience. Talking to the participants and fully understanding their needs will give you additional confidence and an insight into how to adapt your coaching practice to meet each individual's requirements. Attendance at the accompanying workshop will help to reinforce some of the key pointers in this resource, provide additional information, and answer particular queries and concerns.

APPENDIX A

Further Information on Specific Disabilities

Amputees and Les Autres

The British Amputee and Les Autres Sports Association's (BALASA) aim is to provide sporting facilities and opportunities for people with disabilities, particularly for those people who are involved in competitive sport and who are entitled to compete for Great Britain under the International Sports Organisation for the Disabled (ISOD) rules and classification system.

Participants that are in membership of BALASA have locomotor impairments. Individuals with locomotor impairments may have:

- a decrease in muscle strength or function
- motor paralysis of limbs
- a decrease or weakness in joint mobility
- shortening of limbs
- severe reduction of mobility of the back or torso and may have scoliosis.

As far as possible the classification system (including minimal disability) is based on functional ability for each sport. Therefore, an athlete may be eligible for one sporting discipline and not for another.

Amputee Participants

Prospective participants with an amputation are only eligible to compete if they have an amputation that is through or above the wrist or ankle joints.

Les Autres Participants

Participants with locomotor difficulties such as those related to Arthrogryposis, Arthrosis, cerebral palsy (some types), spinal cord conditions (eg polio) multiple sclerosis and muscular dystrophy are allowed to participate in events under the Les Autres classification. Les Autres also incorporates dwarf participants under its classification. The locomotor conditions may be congenital or as a result of injury or accident.

For more information, contact BALASA (address in Appendix E).

Cerebral Palsy

Cerebral palsy is not a disease or illness. It is a brain lesion that is non-progressive and causes variable impairment of the coordination, tone and strength of muscle action impacting on postures and movement. The degree of impairment between individuals with cerebral palsy varies considerably according to the severity and site of the brain damage. No two people with cerebral palsy are alike because the brain damage can evolve differently in each individual. Every individual with cerebral palsy will therefore be different and coaches will need to bear this in mind. Nevertheless, the following points should also be considered. Cerebral palsy:

- is non-fatal, non-contagious, non-progressive but incurable
- has various symptoms according to the location and amount of brain damage
- has a range of symptoms from severe (total inability to control movements) to very mild (some people may have a slight speech impediment)
- results in some individuals having:
  - difficulty in coordinating and integrating basic movement patterns
  - associated impairments such as with vision or hearing, learning disability, epilepsy, speech and language disorders, poor hand-eye control and coordination, or a combination of all these.

Sport can improve cardiovascular function. Coaches who require more information on cerebral palsy are recommended to contact CP Sport (address in Appendix E) or the Cerebral Palsy Helpline 0800-800 3333.

Down's Syndrome and Atlanto-axial Instability

In people with Down's syndrome, the ligaments that normally hold the joints stable can be very slack. People with Down's syndrome may therefore experience a greater range of movement of some joints than the population in general. One of the joints of the neck, the atlanto-axial joint, can be affected. As a result of this and because the actual bones of the joint may be poorly developed, people with Down's syndrome could be more likely to experience a dislocation of the neck. Some research has shown that people who do not have Down's syndrome may also be affected.

It is useful for coaches to be aware of early signs that a health problem may be developing. Look out for:

- pain at a spot near the hard bump behind the ear
- a stiff neck that does not get better quickly
- alteration in the way some people walk so they appear to be less stable on their feet
- deterioration in some people's ability to manipulate things with their hands
- incontinence developing in a person who has previously had no problems.

If any of these occur, the person should consult a doctor. It used to be thought that neck X-rays could identify whether or not the joint is unstable. However, recent investigations have shown this is not always the case. Coaches are recommended to take into consideration the risks involved in their sport in competition and training in relation to participants with or without Down's syndrome, and take precautions necessary to reduce any possibility of neck injury. This may mean consulting with the sport-specific governing body, parents or guardians of participants with Down's syndrome and, of course, the individuals themselves. It is recommended that coaches read *Atlanto-Axial Instability among People with Down's Syndrome*, which can be obtained from the Down's Syndrome Association (address in Appendix E). The leaflet contains the following quote:

> *Life for everyone is not without risk. It is for the individual to decide what risks are acceptable for their children and for themselves. We all have to compromise in our day-to-day lives as we balance freedom to take part in and enjoy life's activities against the risk of possible injury.*
>
> ***Dr Jennifer Dennis***
> ***Medical Adviser to the Down's Syndrome Association***

Hearing Impairments

Damage to the ear can result in hearing loss of one of the following types:

- **Conductive deafness**, which is described as sound not being transmitted well to the inner ear. Winnick (1990) likens it to a radio being turned down low. The sounds are faint but there is no distortion. Conductive deafness can sometimes be corrected.
- **Sensori-neural deafness**, which can be likened to a radio not being tuned in properly (Winnick 1990). There is distortion to the sound as well as the volume. Sound messages are disrupted on their way to the brain.
- **Mixed conductive and sensori-neural deafness**. Some people have a mixed conductive and sensori-neural loss.

Other useful terminology associated with hearing impairment include the following:

- Deafness – a hearing loss that makes it impossible to understand speech through hearing alone, even if a hearing aid is used. There is usually a need for another means of communication such as lip-reading or signing.
- Hearing loss – refers to any problems with understanding normal speech.
- Hard of hearing – this makes the understanding of speech difficult but not impossible.
- Residual hearing – the speech that the individual can understand while wearing a hearing aid.

Hydrocephalus

This is a swelling of the brain caused by a blockage. In everyone, the cerebrospinal fluid (CSF) is produced constantly inside each of the four ventricles (spaces) of the brain. It normally flows from one ventricle to the next, then out over the surface of the brain and down the spinal cord where it is absorbed into the bloodstream. If the drainage pathways are obstructed, CSF accumulates in the ventricles inside the brain causing them to swell.

Excess pressure caused by the blockage can be relieved by the insertion of a shunt which drains excess fluid into the abdominal or heart cavities. Most people born with spina bifida also have hydrocephalus but it can occur independently at birth and later in life. Coaches should be aware of players complaining of headaches and nausea as this may mean there is a shunt blockage or the CSF drainage pathways are obstructed. Medical advice should be sought if this is suspected. Coaches are recommended to contact ASBAH (Association for Spina Bifida and Hydrocephalus) and ask for their leaflet *What is Hydrocephalus?* for more information (address in Appendix D).

Learning Disability

A learning disability is a condition in which the brain does not develop as fast or as fully as it should. The degree of learning disability can vary enormously. It can be caused by several factors but the four most common result from:

- a genetic (inherited) characteristic such as in people with Down's syndrome
- an infection – such as meningitis
- a trauma – for example from an accident at birth, a road traffic accident or a head injury
- social effects – for example as a result of pre-natal influences such as drugs, alcohol, smoking, malnutrition and pollution.

The damage to the brain can cause delay in physical, social, intellectual and emotional development. The performer functions at a level which is less than his chronological age. A learning disability cannot be cured but in many instances, a well structured educational programme, including sports activities, before, during and after school, can help an individual to reach his full potential. However, most individuals will need some sort of support to some degree throughout their lives. Performers with a learning disability have a normal life expectancy but are more likely to suffer from epilepsy and other conditions which can affect life expectancy.

Many people with a learning disability have access to national, international and world-class competition. Contact the UK Sports Association for People with Learning Disability for information about coaching and competition opportunities.

Multiple Sclerosis

This is a condition that affects the central nervous system (CNS). The myelin sheath, a fatty substance covering the nerve fibres which assists the conduction of nerve impulses within the CNS, is scarred by some unknown factor. The scarring prevents or hinders nerve impulses from travelling from the CNS to different parts of the body.

This damage to the CNS can cause difficulty in walking, balance, general coordination and problems with vision, speech, incontinence and weakness, depending on where it occurs. Fatigue is also a common problem. One of the characteristics of multiple sclerosis (MS) is a pattern of remissions and relapses which vary from one person to another. Most people have attacks which may mean new symptoms may appear or old ones worsen. These are followed by periods of complete or partial recovery. A smaller number of people have a progressive course which means the symptoms continue to worsen without remissions. Regular exercise is important to people with MS, but it should be taken according to individual capabilities as over-exertion could cause fatigue which could exacerbate the condition. For more information, contact the Multiple Sclerosis Society of Great Britain and Northern Ireland (address in Appendix E)

Muscular Dystrophy

This refers to a number of conditions that affect the muscle fibres and cause muscle weakness. All the muscular dystrophies are inherited. The most common type of muscular dystrophy is Duchenne. It is rare for girls to inherit this condition, although they can be carriers. Muscular dystrophy is a progressive, degenerative condition which means that an individual's strength and ability will decline over time. In Duchenne muscular dystrophy, the muscles of the heart and chest are affected, as well as those of the back and limbs, and there is usually a progression from walking to using a powered wheelchair. Life expectancy is also shortened in Duchenne muscular dystrophy.

For more information, contact the Muscular Dystrophy Campaign (address in Appendix E).

Post Poliomyelitis Impairment

This condition results from a viral infection affecting the spinal cord leading to temporary or permanent paralysis. The severity and location of paralysis varies between individuals and depends on how the spinal cord has been affected. Players who have had poliomyelitis differ from players who have spinal cord injuries in the following ways:

- Sensation is retained so pain can be felt in the limbs
- Bowel and bladder control is retained
- They are aware of the position of their limbs as messages can be sent back from the limbs to the brain.

Spina Bifida

This occurs in the foetus early on in the pregnancy. It is a fault in the development of the spine which means one or more vertebrae fail to form properly, leaving a gap or split. There are several types of spina bifida. The severe form is Myelomeningocele, where the spinal column is damaged or not properly developed. As a result, there is always some degree of paralysis and loss of sensation below the damaged region. There may be incontinence. Later in life, the spine may curve or twist. Coaches are recommended to contact ASBAH (Association for Spina Bifida and Hydrocephalus) and ask for their leaflet *What is Spina Bifida?* for more information. (Address in Appendix E.)

Spinal Cord Injuries[1]

The spinal cord is the body's means of communication. Running through the bony vertebral (spinal) column, it is made up of nerves which carry messages between the brain and all other parts of the body. A healthy spinal cord will allow uninterrupted communication along its entire column. The sensory nerves will relay messages of feeling and sensation to the brain which will in turn convert them, via motor nerves, into responses such as movements.

If the spinal cord becomes damaged somewhere along its length, the ability to communicate between the brain and the body parts below that point becomes diminished or impossible. If there is an incomplete lesion[2] of the spinal cord, some or all sensation and movement may be retained below the point of injury. A complete lesion will result in total paralysis below the point of injury.

Paraplegia results from a broken back. There will be partial or total paralysis from the chest or waist (depending on the level of lesion) downwards. With normal upper body power and function above the lesion, a person with paraplegia can usually lead an independent lifestyle.

Tetraplegia results from a broken neck. There will be partial or total paralysis of all four limbs. Very high lesions will also affect the diaphragm. In such cases breathing can only be maintained by external mechanical ventilators or by a pacing device. People with tetraplegia, depending upon the level of their lesion may be highly dependent on others for their care.

In both paraplegia and tetraplegia, control of bodily functions (eg bladder, bowels, sexual function) will also be affected.

1 The information pertaining to spinal injuries has been adapted by kind permission of **Back Up**, address in Appendix E.

2 Lesion is the point of damage.

Spinal injury occurs in several ways but mainly through trauma (ie injury) to the fragile nerve fibres of the spinal cord, the most common causes being road traffic accidents and sporting injuries. Less common, though equally damaging are viral infections, viruses, growths and diseases of the spinal cord. Figure 2 shows the spinal column with its various sections and landmarks.

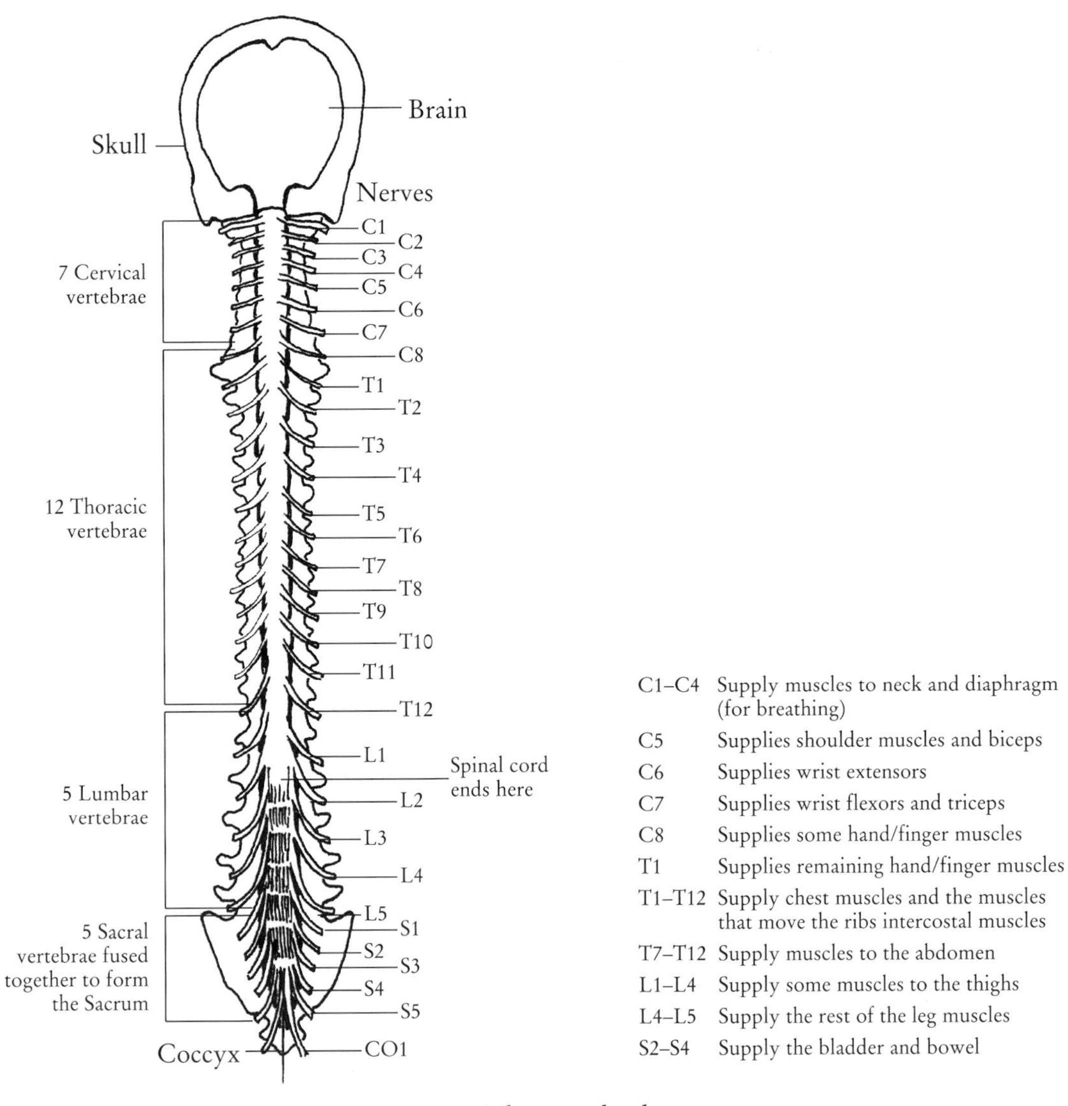

Figure 2: The spinal column
Reproduced with kind permission from Back-up Trust

Visual Impairment

For the purposes of this resource, the term *visual impairment* encompasses those people who are totally blind as well as those who are partially sighted. There are many causes of visual impairment which can generally be categorised as either:

- congenital (present from birth) or
- acquired (occurring after birth as a result of accident, disease or old age).

Whether visual impairment has resulted from a congenital or an acquired cause, the major physical outcome is damage to one or more of the following:

- The eye itself.
- Muscles of the eye.
- Central nervous system.
- Occipital lobe of the brain (the centre for visual identification).
- Optic nerves which relay information from the eye to the brain.

There are various types of impairment:

- Total blindness – the inability to recognise objects or contours in any direction or at any distance.
- Light perception – the ability to distinguish a strong light when it is about one metre from the eye.
- Residual vision – an individual's remaining available vision.

Do not make assumptions about a performer's visual impairment and abilities. Ask the performer to establish the level of vision and any factors that may affect it.

APPENDIX B

Further Information on Specific Health Issues

Asthma

Asthma is a condition in which the breathing tubes or airways (bronchial tubes) in the lungs are narrowed. This happens because the:

- muscles in the airways contract to cause a spasm
- lining of the airway becomes swollen and inflamed
- mucus production is increased in the airways.

These can result from:

- a virus infection such as influenza
- exercise
- sudden changes in temperature
- house dust mite
- an allergic reaction (eg to some food substances, smoke, animal fur)
- excitement and stress
- fumes such as glue or paint.

Although the symptoms of asthma vary from individual to individual, the most common symptoms are coughing, wheezing, chest tightness, difficulty in breathing and tiredness.

Management and treatment

There are three basic approaches:

1. Medication – symptoms of exercise induced asthma may be prevented by taking reliever medication prior to exercise – this cannot guarantee that symptoms will be prevented.
2. Avoidance of trigger factors – it is relatively easy to avoid some trigger factors (such as smoke or animal fur) but in some cases they may be impossible to avoid – for example, exercise induced asthma. Avoiding exercise may prove detrimental to the overall fitness of the individual. Being physically fit can be of great benefit to asthmatics as exercise improves lung capacity.
3. Physical preparation – warm-up exercises such as several 30 second sprints over 5–10 minutes before vigorous games may protect the lungs for an hour or so.

Dealing with an Acute Asthma Attack

1 Encourage the athlete to use the prescribed reliever medication as soon as possible.
2 Never encourage the person to run through an attack.
3 Be aware of the athlete's medical pro forma for details of medication.
4 Help the athlete to relax by keeping calm and avoiding panic. The anxiety caused by the athlete feeling breathless may be made worse if those around are not calm.
5 The medication should take effect in 10–15 minutes. If symptoms do not respond after 2–3 doses of medication, seek medical help immediately.

As a coach working with a performer who has asthma, it is useful to establish how the individual manages her condition, as each individual will have her own strategy. It is recommended that coaches obtain a copy of *Exercise and Asthma* available from the National Asthma Campaign (see address in Appendix E).

Diabetes

Diabetes is a condition in which the body, because of the lack of hormone insulin, is not able to absorb sugar and starch properly. Insulin is one of the hormones that regulates blood glucose concentration levels. It is also involved in the chemical reaction that allows glucose to enter the cells of the body. The glucose in the blood is important as it is essential for normal brain function. If there is not enough insulin, the body cannot use the energy that is contained in the food that is eaten. When this happens, glucose builds up in the blood and overflows into the urine. Generally, injections of insulin help individuals maintain normal blood glucose concentration levels.

Some individuals acquire diabetes later in life – this is known as non-insulin dependent diabetes type 2. It can be managed by healthy eating or a combination of healthy eating, physical activity and appropriate medication and sometimes with insulin injections. If a performer has diabetes, he can check his blood glucose levels by the following procedures:

- Placing a drop of blood on a special chemically impregnated strip and comparing the colour of the strip manually against a strip container.
- Using a blood glucose meter.

If a performer with diabetes is over-exerted, there is a possibility of experiencing abnormal glucose levels or drifting into a diabetic coma. There are two problems with glucose levels which could occur:

Hyperglycaemia (high blood glucose levels) which can occur:

- if not enough insulin medication is taken
- too much food is eaten
- as a result of illness.

The signs are:

- excessive urination and thirst
- itching skin
- slow healing of sores and cuts
- blurred or reduced vision
- increased appetite with weight loss
- easy tiring, drowsiness or fatigue
- headaches
- nausea and sluggishness
- coma, only Type 1 is fatal if left untreated.

Hypoglycaemia (low blood glucose levels) which can occur if:

- too much medication is taken
- meals or snacks are missed
- unplanned physical activities are undertaken.

The signs are:

- hunger, pallor, weakness and perspiration
- mental confusion
- the shakes
- nausea
- changes in behaviour – unusual aggression or quietness
- loss of balance
- blurred or jumpy vision
- sleepiness
- unconsciousness, not normally fatal.

It is unusual for performers to lapse into a coma as symptoms are usually recognised before this. If any of these symptoms are observed, deal with the performer in the way described in the following panel.

Dealing with Diabetes in Emergency Situations

Usually the player with diabetes will be able to tell you he requires rest and over-exertion can be avoided. If this does not occur and the athlete collapses, move to a safe place and keep him warm.

If the athlete is conscious:

- give 3–5 glucose tablets if available (eg Dextrose, Lucozade or the equivalent) or sugar if not (eg a sweet drink (not a diet drink), barley sugar or about seven jelly beans)
- give some starchy carbohydrate foods next (eg sandwiches, biscuits or cereal bar)
- observe the athlete carefully until recovery is complete or help arrives.

If unconscious (fortunately this is rare):

- place the athlete in the recovery position and get medical help immediately. In the case of a child and if appropriate, the messenger should also contact the parents
- do not give the athlete fluid or tablets as this may cause choking
- observe the athlete until medical assistance arrives.

Hazards and contraindications of the involvement of diabetics in physical activity programmes

Hazards

- Successful diabetes management routines should be established before an exercise programme is started. If exercise occurs with a lack of insulin in the blood, the blood sugar will rise during exercise and hyperglycaemia may develop. Those who are newly diagnosed or those having difficulty managing their condition, should be cautious when beginning a training programme.
- An exercise ECG is usually arranged for players with diabetes past the age of 40 years or if the duration of the diabetes exceeds 25 years. Players with diabetes are two or five times more likely to suffer heart and large artery disease than those without diabetes. Consequently, a functional test of their circulation and exercise capacity should be administered. The results of the tests are useful in deciding if their exercise programme should be supervised and for the writing of an exercise prescription.
- Players with diabetes should be encouraged to wear cotton socks, as their feet can become easily damaged.

Contraindications

- Macrovascular disease (disease of the large blood vessels in the body). This includes the vessels supplying the heart, brain and legs. This involves arteriosclerosis (hardening or narrowing of the arteries). It can cause heart disease, peripheral vascular disease (ie poor circulation in the extremities, in particular the feet) and strokes.
- Microvascular disease (disease of the small blood vessels). This includes the nerves, causing a condition known as neuropathy (ie poor sensation, particularly in the feet). This condition may result in an individual being unaware of injuries and consequently the need to treat the injury. It can also affect the eyes, causing retinopathy, a retinal vascular disease which can culminate in haemorrhaging (bleeding) within the retina and blindness. A condition known as nephropathy can be caused in the kidneys whereby wastes can no longer filter out to make urine. In some instances, this can lead to kidney dialysis.

In most instances, diabetes presents no real problems to performers as long as a balance is maintained between:

- food
- medication
- activity.

It is important for the individual players to establish a routine to manage the condition and that as a coach, you are aware of this and what to do in an emergency. Diabetes UK can supply information on all aspects of diabetes including diet and hypoglycaemia (address in Appendix E).

Epilepsy

Epilepsy is a tendency to have recurrent seizures. They may take many forms, differing from one person to another but it is always due to an altered chemical state within the brain. In many cases, the causes of epilepsy are unknown but certain factors can cause seizures such as:

- brain damage
- tumours
- injury or infection.

There are certain factors which may trigger seizures in a susceptible person, such as stress, hormonal changes, lack of sleep, anxiety and lack of food.

There are several kinds of seizures – the most common are:

- generalised absence (used to be called *petit mal*) – the person looks blank and stares for a few seconds, then normal activity will continue
- generalised tonic-clonic (previously called *grand mal*). A common sequence would be stiffening of the body, convulsions, possible blue colour around the mouth. The seizure could last for a few minutes
- complex partial – this involves an altered state of awareness. The person may display strange behaviour or inappropriate actions and may be confused afterwards.

The majority of people with epilepsy have their seizures controlled by anti-epileptic medication. The best way of understanding epilepsy is to speak to the performer concerned and establish how she manages her seizures and what action she would expect you to take. Each person's epilepsy is different. The following panels provide some additional guidance. Coaches who require more information are recommended to contact the British Epilepsy Association (address in Appendix E).

Guidance for coping with a seizure

- No restraints should be applied.
- Do not put anything in the person's mouth.
- The seizure should be allowed to take its course.
- Make the environment safe (ie place a jumper under the person's head, loosen tight clothing, remove electrical goods, sharp objects, glasses and so on). In water environments (ie depending on numbers for lifting and closeness to land, jetties, boats), the performer should be lifted out of the water. If this is not possible, try to support the head above the water. Appropriate buoyancy aids should help and probably keep the individual safer in the water.
- When the seizure has subsided, turn the person onto her side and allow saliva to flow from the mouth and keep the airway open, try to keep the person warm and calm, stay with her and keep her company. Allow the person to rest and monitor her airway, breathing and circulation (ABC).
- Seek medical assistance immediately (ie call an ambulance) if:
  - a seizure lasts for more than five minutes or longer than usual for that person
  - seizures continue one after another without recovery in between
  - the person has injured themselves during the seizure (eg hit head)
  - the person does not have a history of epilepsy (ie it is the first seizure).
- Commence cardiopulmonary resuscitation (CPR) if the person is not breathing normally one minute after the seizure is over.

General Hints for Coaching Players with Convulsive Disorders

- Secure a medical report on all players (ie develop a medical pro forma for all athletes to complete).
- Ask for any information regarding medication and precautionary action and do not disturb the medication schedule.
- Check the athlete's medical needs – particularly if you are travelling for competitions or training camps.
- Remember, fatigue can induce seizures. Develop an appropriate monitoring system between you and the athlete to try to avoid situations where the athlete becomes overtired.
- Monitor athletes with epilepsy closely during cool-down periods as seizures are more likely to occur in this period rather than during the activity itself.
- Avoid rapidly changing environments, flickering lights, flashing lights and strobe lights for people who have photosensitive epilepsy.
- During aquatic activities, it is essential the athlete is supervised at all times.
- Take all precautions with those whose seizures are not medically controlled.
- Be aware that excess alcohol can increase the likelihood of a seizure occurring.
- Some females are more prone to seizures during menstruation.
- Be aware of the information in the panel on coping with a seizure.

APPENDIX C:

The protection of disabled children and vulnerable adults in sport

The information below has been adapted from *Protecting Disabled Children and Adults in Sport and Recreation – the Guide* and is intended to be a basic introduction to the area. Further details can be found on the Child Protection in Sport Unit (CPSU) website or from the English Federation of Disability Sport (EFDS), details in Appendix E.

The Children Act identifies four categories of abuse: neglect, physical, emotional and sexual. Some of the people playing your sport will not be children (The Children Act 1989 describes a child as being under the age of 18 years) but the information is still relevant.

Neglect

- Where an individual is left alone and unsupervised.
- Where a disabled person is exposed to a dangerous situation, for example, because they are unable to see or hear or unable to remove themselves from a situation.

Physical Abuse

- Where a disabled person is forced to take part in a sports activity against their will.
- Where a disabled person is physically restrained in an inappropriate way.

Emotional Abuse

- When disabled people are talked about as if they are not there.
- When a disabled person's self-esteem is undermined through ridicule.

Sexual Abuse

- When disabled people are used by other people to meet their own sexual needs.
- When the disabled person requires personal care, which involves intimate contact with another person, the situation could provide an opportunity for abuse in a seemingly proper context.

It may be useful to remember that all children and adults, regardless of impairment, may be vulnerable at certain times of their lives but for some disabled people, this vulnerability will be more frequent. They could therefore be at higher risk and more open to abuse.

Disabled people can have meaningful relationships with other disabled and non-disabled people. However, if the relationship is with another person in a position of trust, for example, a coach having a sexual relationship with a player, then refer to the sport's NGB procedures for guidance.

It may also be useful to be aware of procedures to follow if bullying is suspected. Attendance at a *Good Practice and Child Protection* workshop is recommended for further information and guidance in all of the above areas. For details of workshops in your area, telephone **sports coach UK** on 0113-274 4802, or find details of your local regional office on the website at www.sportscoachuk.org

APPENDIX D

Brief History of Disabled Sport and Present Structure

It is generally considered that sport for disabled people has developed largely this century with the introduction in 1948 of competition for wheelchair athletes at Stoke Mandeville Hospital, Aylesbury. The first International Wheelchair Games were organised by Sir Ludwig Guttmann, a neurosurgeon, to coincide with the London Olympics. This was done in an attempt to give the Games the same status as the Olympic Games. A deliberate attempt to connect the Olympics and Paralympics (Parallel Olympics) was not made again until 1960 in Rome. Since that time, the Paralympics have been held every four years. Table 3 shows some of the cities and countries which have hosted the Olympic Games.

Table 1: Cities and Countries which have hosted the Paralympic Games

Year	City	Country	Olympics
1960	Rome	Italy	Rome
1964	Tokyo	Japan	Tokyo
1968	Tel Aviv	Israel	Mexico
1972	Heidelberg	Germany	Munich
1976	Toronto	Canada	Montreal
1980	Arnhem	Holland	Moscow[1]
1984	Stoke Mandeville England and Nassau County, New York	USA	
1988	Seoul	Korea	Seoul[2]
1992	Barcelona	Spain	Barcelona
1996	Atlanta	USA	Atlanta
2000	Sydney	Australia	Sydney

1 The Soviet Union, at that time, said it had no disabled citizens and would consequently be unable to hold the Paralympic Games.

2 Seoul is generally acknowledged to be the first, *modern* Paralympics. The Koreans had no background in disability sport and just chose to *parallel* the Olympic arrangements.

The Winter Paralympics are held every four years, the first Games being held in 1990 in France, the 1994 Games being held in Lillehammer in Norway, the 1998 Games in Nagano, Japan and most recently the 2002 games held in Salt Lake City. However, disabled performers have competed in demonstration events in several previous Winter Olympics. Like the Paralympics, the Winter Paralympics are the pinnacle of competition for elite athletes with physical disabilities.

Initially, the Paralympics only catered for athletes who used wheelchairs but gradually, as the Paralympic movement grew, other classes of athletes began to participate. In 1982 the International Co-ordinating Committee of World Sports Organisation for the Disabled (ICC) was established as a counterpart to the International Olympic Committee. The ICC had four International Federations under its umbrella:

- Cerebral Palsy International Sports and Recreation Association (CP-ISRA)
- International Blind Sports Association (IBSA)
- International Stoke Mandeville Wheelchair Sports Foundation (ISMWSF)
- International Sports Organisation for the Disabled (ISOD). This organisation governs amputees as well as Les Autres Performers.

In 1992 the ICC was restructured and became the International Paralympic Committee (IPC). The International Sports Organisations organise competition for their own specific disability groups. For more information, contact the national disability sports organisations (NDSO) – the address can be found in Appendix E. As the Paralympic Movement has developed over the years, performers with learning disability have been integrated into events. The International Federation of Sport for People with Intellectual Disability (INAS-FID) is universally recognised as representing the interests of performers with a learning disability and is a member of the IPC. As well as working towards the integration of performers with a learning disability into the Paralympics, INAS-FID has also organised other events, for example, World Championships in athletics, basketball, table tennis, swimming and football. INAS-FID ensured that the Sydney Paralympics in 2000 widened the programme of competition for people with learning disability. The Special Olympics movement was founded in 1968 by Eunice Kennedy Shriver to enable people with a learning disability to compete together. The emphasis of the Special Olympics movement is on giving individuals the opportunity to compete in the sports of their choice, regardless of ability, each individual athlete being matched to other athletes of similar ability for competition. However, the Special Olympics movement is structured for participation more than for elite performance. In this way it differs significantly from the Paralypic and INAS-FID movements.

The World Games for the Deaf have been held regularly since the first games in 1924 in Paris. The games are held every four years in the year following the Olympic year. The games are not only concerned with competition but are also a celebration of deaf culture. For more information on the development of sport for particular disability groups, contact the appropriate NDSO (addresses in Appendix E).

Development of the Paralympic Movement

1948	First competition for athletes with a disability, Stoke Mandeville
1952	First international competition for athletes with a spinal cord lesion
1976	Amputees included in international games
1980	Blind athletes and the Les Autres group join the Paralympic movement
1984	Athletes with Cerebral Palsy compete in Paralympics
1992	Athletes with learning difficulties included (separate event)
1996	Integration of athletes with learning difficulties

Organisations that coordinate sport for people with disabilities

National coordination of international multi-disciplinary competition/activity

British Paralympic Association (BPA)

UK/home country sports associations

United Kingdom Sports Association for People with Learning Disability (UKSAPLD)

English Federation of Disability Sport (EFDS – England)

Federation of Sports Associations for the Disabled (FSAD – Wales)

Scottish Association for the Disabled (SSAD)

Northern Ireland Committee on Sport for People with Disabilities

National disability sports organisations

British Wheelchair Sports Foundation (BWSF)

Cerebral Palsy Sport (CP Sport)

British Amputee and Les Autres Sports Association (BALASA)

British Blind Sport (BBS)

British Deaf Sports Council (BDSC)

English Sports Association for People with a Learning Disability (ESAPLD)

Disability Sport England

Other Organisations

Mini Olympics

Special Olympics

Gateway/Mencap

National sport-specific disability organisations

For example:

The Great Britain Wheelchair Rugby Association (GBWRA) is an associate member of BWSF.

Great Britain Basketball Association, Riding for the Disabled, English Table Tennis Association for the Disabled, RYA Sailability.

English Federation of Disability Sport (EFDS)

The EFDS was formally established in 1998 as an umbrella body to lead a unified, coordinated and comprehensive approach to sports development in England for disabled people.

The EFDS brings together a number of established national and regional agencies with complementary roles. The national agencies are the seven national disability sports organisations (NDSOs) described above. These are involved in elite level competitive sporting structures including national and international championships and have their own development programmes.

At a regional level, there are ten regional federations who coordinate and support the delivery of grass roots development by working closely with other local agencies to encourage participation.

Contact details can be found in Appendix E.

APPENDIX E

Useful Addresses and Contacts

For the UK

Association for Spina Bifida and Hydrocephalus (ASBAH)
ASBAH House
42 Park Rd
Peterborough
PE1 2UQ
Tel: 01733-555988
Fax: 01733-555985
E-mail:
postmaster@asbah.org
Website:
www.asbah.org

British Amputee & Les Autres Sports Association
30 Greaves Close
Arnold
Nottingham
NG5 6RS
Tel and Fax: 0115-926 0220
E-mail:
balasa@ic24.net
Website:
www.chap14.freeserve.co.uk/balasa1/

British Deaf Sports Council
43 Swarcliffe Avenue
Swarcliffe
Leeds LS14 5LF
Voice: 01943-850214
DCT: 01943-850081
Fax: 01943-850828
E-mail:
enquiries@britishdeafsportscouncil.org.uk
Website:
www.britishdeafsportscouncil.org.uk

Back-Up Trust
The Business Village
Broomhill Road
Wandsworth
London
SW18 4JQ
Tel: 020-8875 1805
Fax: 020-8870 3619
E-mail:
admin@backuptrust.org.uk
Website:
www.backuptrust.org.uk

British Blind Sport
4–6 Victoria Terrace
Royal Leamington Spa
Warwickshire
CV31 3AB
Telephone: 08700-789000
Fax: 08700-789001
E-mail:
info@britishblindsport.org.uk
Website:
www.britishblindsport.org.uk

Diabetes UK
10 Parkway
London
NW1 7AA
Tel: 020-7424 1000
Fax: 020-7424 1001
E-mail:
info@diabetes.org.uk
Website:
www.diabetes.org.uk

British Epilepsy Association
New Anstey House
Gate Way Drive
Yeadon
Leeds
LS19 7XY
Tel: 0113-201 8800
Fax: 0113-390 0300
E-mail:
epilepsy@epilepsy.org.uk
Website:
www.epilepsy.org.uk

British Wheelchair Sports Foundation
Guttmann Road
Stoke Mandeville
Buckinghamshire
HP21 9PP
Tel: 01296-395995
Fax: 01296-424171
E-mail:
enquiries@britishwheelchairsports.org
Website:
www.britishwheelchairsports.org

CP Sport
Suite 32
Trent Bridge Cricket Centre
Notts County Cricket Club
Trenty Bridge
Nottingham
NG2 6AG
Tel: 0115-982 5352/58
Fax: 0115-981 5484
E-mail:
info@cpsport.org
Website:
www.cpsport.org

British Paralympic Association
Norwich Union Building
9th Floor
69 Park Lane
Croydon
CR9 1BG
Tel: 020-7662 8882
Fax: 020-7662 8310
E-mail:
info@paralympics.org.uk
Website:
www.paralympics.org.uk

Central Council of Physical Recreation
Francis House
Francis Street
London
SW1P 1DE
Tel: 020-7854 8500
Fax: 020-7854 8501
E-mail: info@ccpr.org.uk
Website: www.ccpr.org.uk

Down's Syndrome Association
155 Mitcham Road
London
SW17 9PG
Tel: 020-8682 4001
Fax: 020-8682 4012
E-mail:
info@downs-syndrome.org.uk
Website:
www.dsa-uk.com

National Deaf Children's Society
15 Dufferin Street
London
EC1Y 8UR
Tel: 020-7490 8656
Minicom: 020-7490 8656
Fax: 020-7251 5020
E-mail:
ndcs@ndcs.org.uk
Website:
www.ndcs.org.uk

Mini Olympics
23 Mansfields
Writtle
Chelmsford
Essex
CM1 3NH
Tel: 01245-420041

Multiple Sclerosis Society
MS National Centre
375 Edgware Road
London
NW2 6ND
Tel: 020-8438 0700
Fax: 020-8438 0701
E-mail:
info@mssociety.org.uk
Website:
www.mssociety.org.uk

Muscular Dystrophy Group of Great Britain and Northern Ireland
7–11 Prescott Place
London
SW4 6BS
Tel: 020-7720 8055
Fax: 020-7498 0670
E-mail:
info@muscular-dystrophy.org
Website:
www.muscular-dystrophy.org

National Asthma Campaign
Providence House
Providence Place
London
N1 0NT
Telephone: 020-7226 2260
Fax: 020-7704 0470
Website:
www.asthma.org.uk

National Federation of Gateway Clubs
123 Golden Lane
London
EC1Y 0RT
Tel: 020-7454 0454 (Helpline)
/020-7696 5521 (Admin)
Fax: 020-7608 3254

Physically Handicapped and Able Bodied
Summit House
50 Wandle Road
Croydon
CR0 1DF
Tel: 020-8667 9443
Fax: 020-8681 1399
E-mail:
info@phabengland.org.uk
Website:
www.phabengland.org.uk

Royal National Institute for the Deaf
19–23 Featherstone St
London
EC1Y 8SL
Tel: 020-7296 8000
Fax: 020-7296 8199
Textphone: 020-7296 8001
E-mail:
informationline@rnid.org.uk
Website:
www.rnid.org.uk

Special Olympics GB
Lower Ground Floor
4 St Johns Road
Tunbridge Wells
Kent
TN4 9ET
Tel: 01892-540484/545810
Fax: 01892-545247
E-mail:
info@specialolympicsgb.org
Website:
www.specialolympicsgb.org

United Kingdom Sports Association for People with Learning Disability (UKSAPLD)
UK Sports Association
Leroy House
436 Essex Road
London N1 3QP
Tel: 020-7354 1030
Fax: 020-7354 2593
E-mail:
office@uksapld.freeserve.co.uk

sports coach UK
114 Cardigan Road
Headingley
Leeds
LS6 3BJ
Tel: 0113-274 4802
Fax: 0113-275 5019
E-mail:
coaching@sportscoachuk.org
Website:
www.sportscoachuk.org

Makaton (MVDP)
31 Firwood Drive
Camberley
Surrey
GU15 3QD
Tel: 01276-61390
Fax: 01276-681368
E-mail:
mvdp@makaton.org
Website:
www.makaton.org

For England

EFDS Head Office:
Manchester Metropolitan University
Alsager Campus
Hassall Road
Alsager
ST7 2HL
Tel: 0161-247 5294
Fax: 0161-247 5644
Minicom number: 0161-247 5644
E-mail:
federation@efds.co.uk
Website:
www.efds.net

Disability Sport England
Solecast House
13–27 Brunswick Place
London
N1 6DX
Tel: 020 7190 4919
Fax: 020-7490 4914

Sport England
16 Upper Woburn Place
London
WC1H 0QP
Tel: 020-7273 1500
Fax: 020-7383 5740
E-mail:
info@sportengland.org
Website:
www.sportengland.org

English Sports Association for People with Learning Disabilities
Unit 9
Milner Way
Ossett
WF5 9JN
Tel: 01924-267555
Fax: 01924-267666
E-mail:
info@esapld.co.uk
Website:
www.esapld.co.uk

Child Protection in Sport Unit (CPSU)
NSPCC National Training Centre
3 Gilmour Close
Beaumont Leys
Leicester
LE4 1EZ
Tel: 0116-234 7278/7280
Fax: 0116-234 0464
E-mail:
cpsu@nspcc.org.uk
Website:
www.sportprotects.co.uk

For Northern Ireland

Disability Action
2 Annadale Ave
Belfast
BT7 3JH
Tel: 01232-322504

Northern Ireland Sports Council
House of Sport
Upper Malone Road
Belfast
BT9 5LA
Tel: 028-90 381222
Fax: 028-90 682757
E-mail:
info@sportni.net
Website:
www.sportni.net

For Wales

Disability Sport Wales
Sophia Gardens
Cardiff
CF1 9SW
Tel: 029-2030 0500
Fax: 029-2030 0600

Federation of Sports Association for the Disabled
Whitehaven
Blaenavon Road
Govilon
Abergavenny
NP7 9NY
Tel: 01873-830533
Fax: 01873-830533

The Sports Council for Wales
Welsh Institute of Sport
Sophia Gardens
Cardiff
CF1 9SW
Tel: 029-2030 0500
Fax: 029-2030 0600
E-mail:
scw@scw.co.uk
Website:
www.sports-council-wales.co.uk

For Scotland

Scottish Sports Association for Disabled People
FIPRE
Viewfield Road
Glenrothes
Fife
KY6 2RA
Tel: 01592-415700
Fax: 01592-415710

Sportscotland
Caledonia House
South Gyle
Edinburgh
EH12 9DQ
Tel: 0131-317 7200
Fax: 0131-317 7202
Website:
www.sportscotland.org.uk

sports coach UK Workshops and Resources

Recommended **scUK** workshops and resources (complimentary with the corresponding workshop) include:

scUK Develop Your Coaching Workshop	Accompanying Resource
A Guide to Mentoring Sports Coaches	A Guide to Mentoring Sports Coaches
Analysing Your Coaching	Analysing Your Coaching
Coaching and the Law	–
Coaching Children and Young People	Coaching Young Performers
Coaching Disabled Performers	Coaching Disabled Performers
Coaching Methods and Communication	The Successful Coach
Equity in Your Coaching	Equity in Your Coaching
Field Based Fitness Testing	A Guide to Field Based Fitness Testing
Fitness and Training	Physiology and Performance
Fuelling Performers	Fuelling Performers
Goal-setting and Planning	Planning Coaching Programmes
Good Practice and Child Protection	Protecting Children
Imagery Training	Imagery Training
Improving Practices and Skill	Improving Practices and Skill
Injury Prevention and Management	Sports Injury
Motivation and Mental Toughness	Motivation and Mental Toughness
Observation, Analysis and Video	Observation, Analysis and Video
Performance Profiling	Performance Profiling
The Responsible Sports Coach	–
Understanding Eating Disorders	–

Details of all **scUK** resources are available from:

Coachwise 1st4sport
Chelsea Close
Off Amberley Road
Armley
Leeds
LS12 4HP
Tel: 0113-201 5555
Fax: 0113-231 9606
E-mail: enquiries@1s4sport.com
Website: www.1st4sport.com

scUK also produces a technical journal – Faster, Higher, Stronger (FHS) and an information update service for coaches (**sports coach update**). Details of these services are available from:

sports coach UK
114 Cardigan Road
Headingley
Leeds
LS6 3BJ
Tel: 0113-274 4802
Fax: 0113-275 5019
E-mail: coaching@sportscoachuk.org
Website: www.sportscoachuk.org

For general information about **sports coach UK** workshops, contact the Workshop Booking Centre on 0845-601 3054. For details of workshops running in your area, contact your nearest Regional Training Unit (RTU) or home countries office or visit www.sportscoachuk.org. RTU details are available on the **sports coach UK** website.

APPENDIX F

References

BAALPE (1989) **Physical education for children with special educational needs in mainstream education.** ISBN 1 871228 03 4.

De Pauw, KP and Gavron, SJ (1995) **Disability and sport.** Champaign IL, Human Kinetics. ISBN 0 873228 48 0.

Wade, B and Moore, M (1992) **Experiencing special education: what young people with special needs can tell us.** Milton Keynes, Open University Press. ISBN 0 335096 79 4.

sports coach UK (1999) **The successful coach: guidelines for coaching practice.** Leeds, **sports coach UK.** ISBN 0 947850 16 3.

(1995) **Wolfe's medical dictionary.** London, Wolfe. ISBN 0 723418 36 5.

APPENDIX G

Further Reading

Books

BAALPE (1996) **Physical education for children with special educational needs in mainstream education**. Leeds, White Line Press. ISBN 1 871228 03 4.

Braggins, A (1994) **Trail orienteering: An outdoor activity for people with disabilities**. British Orienteering Federation, Harvey Map Series. ISBN 1 851370 90 0.

BT Countryside for All: Good Practice Guide. Fieldfare Trust. Tel: 0114-270 1668 Website: www.fieldfare.org.uk.

Brown, A (1987) **Active games for children with movement problems**. Thousand Oaks CA, Sage Publications. ISBN 1 853961 48 5.

DePauw, KP and Gavron, SJ (1995) **Disability and sport**. Champaign IL, Human Kinetics. ISBN 0 873228 48 0.

Goldberg, B (1995) **Sport and exercise for children with chronic health conditions**. Champaign IL, Human Kinetics. ISBN 0 87322 873 1.

Kasser, S L (1995) **Inclusive games movement fun for everyone**. Champaign IL, Human Kinetics. ISBN 0 87322 639 9.

Kerr, A and Stafford, I (2003) **How to coach disabled people in sport**. Leeds, **sports coach** UK. ISBN 1 902523 54 7.

Lockette, K and Keys, A (1994) **Conditioning with physical disabilities**. Champaign IL, Human Kinetics. ISBN 0 873226 14 3.

Male, J and Thompson, C (1985) **The educational implications of disability – A guide for teachers**. London, Radar. ISBN 0 900270 37 3.

Pointer, B (1992) **Movement activities for children with learning difficulties**. London, Jessica Kingsley Publishers. ISBN 1 853021 67 9.

Rappaport Morris, L and Schulz, L (1989) **Creative play activities for children with disabilities**. Champaign IL, Human Kinetics. ISBN 0 873229 33 9.

Smedley, G (1999) **Canoeing for disabled people**. Leicester, British Canoe Union. ISBN 0 900082 08 9.

String, T and Le Fevre, D (1999) **Parachute games**. Oxfam Educational. ISBN 0 873227 93 X.

Wing, L (1996) **Autistic children: A guide for parents and professionals**. London, Citadel Press. ISBN 0 806504 08 0.

Winnicks, JP (ed) (2000) **Adapted physical education and sport**. Champaign IL, Human Kinetics. ISBN 0 736033 24 6.

Awards

The Duke of Edinburgh Award Scheme
Gulliver House
Madeira Walk
Windsor
Berkshire
SL4 1EU
Tel: 01753-727400
E-mail: info@theaward.org
Website: www.theaward.org

The Gateway Award
Tel: 0121-707 7877
E-mail: gateway.award@mencap.org.uk
Website: www.mencap.org.uk/html/gateway

Newspapers and Magazines

Access by Design
Access by Design is the leading UK publication with a focus on design, disability and access to the built environment. Published quarterly, *Access by Design* regularly features: design sheets, building studies, updates on legislation, reports on current research and book reviews.

Available from:
Centre for Accessible Environments
Nutmeg House
60 Gainsford Street
London
SE1 2NY
Tel: 0171-357 8182
Website: www.cae.org.uk

Disability Now
The UK's leading disability magazine and website, giving essential information: news and feature articles, advice, adverts, links, an archive and a chat forum.

For a free introductory copy:
Tel: 0845-120 7001 or
E-mail: dnsubs@cisubs.co.uk
Website: www.disabilitynow.org.uk

Also available on cassette, disk or via e-mail from Talking Newspapers Enterprises Ltd (Tel: 01435-862737).

Disability Times

Disability Times is a campaigning and equal opportunities newspaper, which is produced not for profit, mostly by disabled people.

Available from:
84 Claverton Street
London
SW1V 3AX
Tel and Fax: 020-7233 7970
Disability Times is also on Channel 4 Teletext p686

Inclusive Sport

The magazine profiles a wide range of sporting opportunities available to disabled people and is packed full of useful and interesting information across all areas of Disability Sport.

If you would like further information or wish to subscribe to *Inclusive Sport* contact:
English Federation of Disability Sport
Manchester Metropolitan University
Alsager Campus
Hassall Road
Alsager
Stoke on Trent
ST7 2HL
Tel: 0161-247 5294
Fax: 0161-247 6895
Minicom: 0161-247 5644
E-mail: federation@efds.co.uk
Website: www.efds.net

Link Magazine

ASBAH produces a bi-monthly magazine, which has a worldwide circulation to people with spina bifida and/or hydrocephalus and their families, schools, hospitals, research centres, journalists and other groups of professionals.

Available from:
Publicity
Asbah House
42 Park Rd
Peterborough
PE1 2UQ
Tel: 01733-555988
E-mail: link@asbah.org
Website: www.asbah.org

Red Herring
14 First Avenue
Dursley
Gloucester
GL11 4NW
Tel: 01453-543347

Remploy News
415 Edgeware Rd
Cricklewood
London
NW1 6LR
Tel: 0800-138 7656
Fax: 0800-138 7657
Website: www.remploy.co.uk

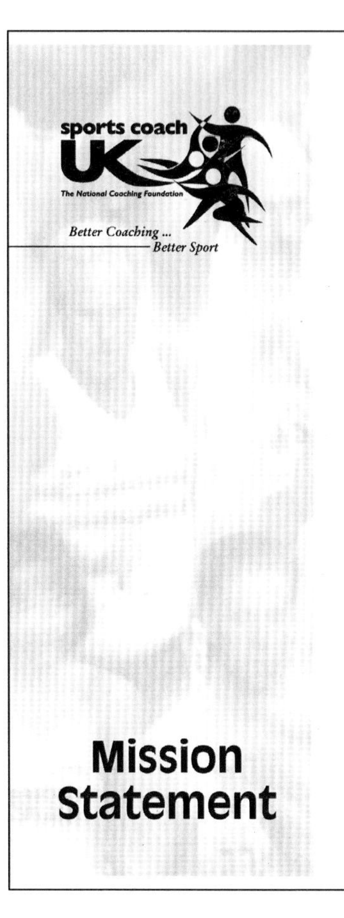

sports coach UK is dedicated to guiding the development and implementation of a coaching system, recognised as a world leader, for coaches at every level in the UK.

We will work with our partners to achieve this by promoting:

- ✓ professional and ethical values and inclusive and equitable practice
- ✓ agreed national standards of competence as a benchmark at all levels
- ✓ a regulated and licensed structure
- ✓ recognition, value and appropriate funding and reward
- ✓ a culture and structure of innovation, constant renewal and continuous professional development.